AUGUST 2022 EDITION

AN ANTHOLOGY OF ARTICLES

BRILLOPEDIA

Contents

Preface

"Start writing, no matter what. The water does not flow until the faucet is turned on".

- Louis L'Amour

This book is a bouquet of articles contributed by students, professors and academicians. Hundreds of students and professors are contributing their work to Brillopedia, we are here to provide ample information about Law and Contemporary issues. Our aim is to provide a platform for today's generation to express their views and ideas on law and contemporary law.

CHAPTER ONE

ANALYSIS OF RAPE REGULATIONS IN INDIA

Author: Deep Kathin, V Year of B.L.S.,LL.B from Rizvi Law College/ Mumbai University.

Abstract

Rape is a heinous and intrusive act. It has the power to transform the victim's life completely. When a crime is committed, the victim may be able to go on with their life. In the case of rape victims, however, this is not the case. After the incident, the victim will have to deal with a slew of other concerns. Many rape victims suffer long-term ramifications as a result of their ordeal. Rape laws in India have been a source of contention for a long time, but following the Delhi rape case event, the debate heated up, resulting in significant modifications to the country's rape laws. In India, rape rules are enshrined in the Indian penal code, which was enacted in 1860. Since then, the situation has altered dramatically as the crimes have become more terrible and the number of incidents has risen dramatically. Rape, the most terrible crime, continues to occur at an alarming rate in our culture. Even after new laws have been implemented, the condition has not improved; in fact, it has gotten worse, as the number of instances has skyrocketed, despite the fact that the majority of incidents continue to go unreported owing to societal pressure. One of the primary questions that need to be addressed is why, despite so many changes in the legislation, victims of rape are stigmatized by society and the system. The study examines the Indian legal system in relation to rape, focusing on sections 375 and 376 of the Indian Penal Code, 1860.

Keywords: - Rape, Voyeurism, Disrobing, Girl Child, Prostitution.

Introduction

Rape is a violent crime that many women see as life-threatening conduct that leaves them feeling terrified and humiliated. Sexual offenses, such as rape, are a distinct type of crime that arises from a man's wrongdoing and destructive thinking. Rape is defined as the use of force against a woman without her consent, whether through fear or deception. Rape, in general, is the material knowledge of any woman when she reaches puberty, against her will, or of a woman's child, with or without her consent, when she is under the age of puberty. 33,356 rape crimes were registered in India in 2018, according to the National Crime Records Bureau's (NCRB) 2018 periodic report.

India's rape laws aren't completely accurate. India has been recognized as one of the countries having the highest rates of rape per capita. A guy commits rape only when he engages in sexual activity with a woman. Under many conditions, a woman may be dragged against her will and engage in sexual activity with a male without her consent. The woman is pushed to the point where she is threatened with murder, and in many cases, killing occurs. In certain situations, the woman is drugged to the point that she gets captivated and loses her mind, rendering her incapable of comprehending the nature and repercussions of what she agrees to with the male. Rape is one of the most serious issues confronting people all over the world. India is one of the countries that is known as the world's rape capital. Rape is a growing problem in today's culture, and it's becoming increasingly difficult to ignore the awful statistics surrounding incidents. In India, this is the fastest-growing crime. According to the most recent data from 2018, India ranks third in the world for rape occurrences.

Social Impact and problems faced by the victim

In India, the victim of rape is the most traumatized, and society, rather than encouraging the victim, often humiliates them. The majority of rape incidents in India go unreported due to the victim's stigma.

Rape is particularly stigmatizing; a rape victim (specifically one who was formerly a virgin) may well be perceived as "damaged" by society. Victims may be isolated, have friends and relatives abandon them, be barred from marrying, divorced if it was already married, or perhaps even killed.

The following are some of the issues that rape victims face

1. Restriction of one's rights to life and personal liberty
2. Forced to go through painful processes and questions from both inside and outside the court.

3. Society has shunned them, and they have been denied the right to an education at times.
4. Attempting to make her a controversial figure has resulted in her being exploited by the media and the persons involved.
5. Various political parties interfering in the problem or making it a political issue.
6. The victim is denied access to certain rehabilitative and maintenance services.
7. Delay in the trial process, resulting in a delay in the delivery of justice.
8. Difficulty on the part of the investigative agency in identifying the true perpetrators.

Furthermore, women are frequently harassed by police personnel when filing a First Information Report and by doctors during medical examinations; victims are sometimes tormented by authorities to the point of suicide. According to research, 6% of raped high school girls attempted suicide. Rape as well as other types of sexual assault on children can cause short- and long-term harm, as well as psychopathology later in life. Depression, post-traumatic stress disorder, anxiety, disordered eating, low self-esteem, post-traumatic- traumatic stress, and mental illnesses; general psychological problems and abnormalities such as somatization, neurosis, chronic pain, sexualized behaviour, school/learning problems; and behaviour problems such as substance abuse, destructive behaviour, criminality, and suicide are among the psychological, emotional, physical, and social effects.

The MATHURA RAPE CASE is yet another label for it. A 16-year-old girl from the "Mathura" tribal community was raped by two police officers in a police station in this case. Following that, the family members filed a criminal complaint against the cops involved. The Supreme Court of India, on the other hand, dismissed the case, finding that "Mathura's body displayed no visible signs of rape." This verdict has sparked a massive movement among numerous women's organizations across the country. Four eminent law professors addressed an open letter to the Chief Justice of India challenging this decision in a row. After this incident, a criminal law amendment was made in response to the entire occurrence. The following are the key elements of the amendment in 1973:

1. The term "custodial rape" had been coined for the first time.
2. Closed proceedings for the rape trials.

3. It is also prohibited to reveal the identity of victims.

The State of Maharashtra vs. Madhukar is another case. Madhukar, a police inspector, had come on the door of one Banubi's hut late at night and intended to be physical with her. However, when she heard her neighbor and husband arriving, she began shouting. The inspector was fired as a result of her complaint. However, following the initial investigation, it was discovered that Banubi was a "lady of easy virtue." On the police inspector's appeal, the High Court took into account Banubi's easy virtue and ruled in favor of the inspector. According to the Supreme Court, a woman of easy virtue has the right to privacy, and no one has the authority to invade her privacy at any time. As a result, no one has the right to violate a female person whenever he wants. If someone tries to violate her privacy against her will, she has the right to defend herself. She is also entitled to legal protection. As a result, her evidence cannot be tossed overboard simply because she is a woman of easy virtue.

Rape is clearly a heinous crime that causes significant trauma to the victim. Rape victims are almost always women. A woman's body is not her property, and no person has any right to touch her unless she consents. Following the Nirbhaya Rape case, in which a woman was brutally raped while out late at night, our government has made steps to remediate the situation and enforce existing laws. It has been observed that the judiciary, as the third pillar of the Constitution, has played a critical role in rape cases. After the horrifying Delhi Gang Rape case, which stunned the entire nation with the ferocity of the deed perpetrated, the Criminal Law Amendment Act of 2013 was enacted. The legislature was forced to consider revising the current rape laws due to widespread demonstrations and agitation. The primary objective was to make them stricter and impose heavier penalties, as well as to widen the scope and interpretation of the word "rape". The Late 'Justice Verma Committee,' which included late Justice J.S.Verma, Gopal Subramaniam, and ex-Justice Leila Seth, was formed to collect opinions and make a recommendation for the legislature to draught legislation to counter rape and other crimes against women. The special committee was so vigorous in its work that it obtained as many as 80,000 recommendations for consideration during its brief existence. Activists, attorneys, NGOs, and other representatives of the alleged "civil society" sent these recommendations. The committee's recommendations were introduced through an ordinance because the legislature was adjourned and there was no session.

The crime of rape has now been altered or given a wider definition that encompasses any type of penetration as well as any portion of a woman's or girl's body. This was the most significant alteration, as previously, Penile Vaginal Penetration was only defined as rape under section 375 of the IPC. From police stations to courtrooms, victims are harassed at every opportunity. Every stage of the victims' battle for justice, from the poor healthcare system to the criminal enforcement system, adds to their agony. The society in which we live plays a critical role in obstructing access to justice. As a result, the full impact of the legislation will never be accomplished unless and until societal change occurs concurrently with legislative reforms.

<u>Conclusion</u>

With rapid changes in the socio-economic structure of society, India's condition has evolved dramatically in the recent decade. The structure of offenses committed in India has altered as a result of the clash between new generation thinking and previous generations' conventional thinking. The necessity for judicial awareness, as well as a shift in thinking and mentality, is urgent. Persons are being educated to see women as people, not commodities, and to advocate and enforce women's rights. Women's safety should not be left solely in the hands of the police, but should also be the duty of the general population. Changes need to be made not only within the legislation but also in people's thoughts, such that rape victims are no longer stigmatized. To ensure that rape victims are never longer abused, changes need to be made not only to the legislation but also to the public's mindset. Laws may have become more rigorous in the aftermath of the occurrence, but enforcement remains a problem on the ground, with the number of instances increasing year after year.

CHAPTER TWO

LIVE-IN-RELATIONSHIP IN INDIA: A CONCEPT ON RISE

Author: Shriyanshi, II Year of B.A.,LL.B(Hons.) From Amity University Lucknow.

ABSTRACT

After getting ruled for almost a century by the Britishers, it was quite evident that the framers of the Constitution would give their country, their beloved motherland a long-written book that would contain all the laws regarding the rights and the duties and differentiating between the legislature, executive and judiciary. The most pious part, the basic structure, the Preamble, everything that would guarantee a smooth functioning of all the three parts of the administration yet they might have not foreseen the circumstances that would arise after the influence of the western winds, that is, the concept of live-in-relationship. It is often a debated topic as it has no laws or legislation surrounding it. The cohabitation is condemned across the whole country because of the social unacceptance and the narrow-minded thinking of the individuals, though there have been pronouncements by the Supreme Court in various cases still this concept is considered a taboo and a social evil. This researcher paper looks into the issues revolving around this taboo as named by the society, why it is condemned on a large scale, its legality in India and abroad, the issues that stop the society from accepting it, the pros and cons surrounding, the recent take of the apex court on this issue.

INTRODUCTION

Robert H. Lawie defined marriage, "Marriage is a relatively permanent bond between permissible mates." Marriage is a social recognition; it brings two people and families of two people together and their relationship is given approval from the society after having blessed with their particular religions' rituals and traditions. It is considered as a universal concept, contributes to emotional and intellectual interstimulation of the partners and aims at social solidarity. It is different in different society with different culture but is recognized and considered an institution.

Marriage has been widely described by many sociologists, psychologists and other eminent people, it also has laws and regulations governing it. No doubt it is one of the most important parts of life and leads to the development of the society but when we look on the other side of the coin wherein the equation is completely different: cohabitation, "a living arrangement in which an unmarried couple lives together in a long-term relationship that ensembles marriage."

Cohabitation is living with each other of opposite sex without any legal rights imposing on both of them. It is often seen in the western countries but has soon covered the whole of the world. It is considered an option by the woman to see if the partner is compatible and by men to see if he can give lifetime commitment, it is like living without marriage and whether they can adjust to it. There are a group of people who we see supporting this concept but many stand against it as it is against the normal flow of the life or it does not legal implication or acceptance by the society but we cannot ignore either side's argument because it is as obvious to have both the sides of the coin because premarital cohabitation can lead to issues such as increase in divorce rates as the partner are not committed to each other. As was held by the co- director of the Centre for Marital and Family Studies at the University of Denver, Stanley that it is a relationship "inertia".

"Men and women who moved in together used to raise eyebrows. Living together out of wedlock, once considered "shacking up" or "living in sin," has lost its stigma as cohabitation has become mainstream."

"Cohabitation research published in the journal Population Studies in 2000 found that within five years of a live-in relationship, about half of couples married, about 40% split up and the rest continued to live together." These findings only reveal the amount of people getting successful after cohabitation but that does not mean the live-ins should be discarded and thrown out of the community, we cannot stop others from doing what is best for their relationship just on the basis of these figures.

It is up to the individuals to decide for themselves because every country has given in its part the freedom to do take choice for oneself and the same goes for India too but since our land is considered to be the sacred, these things will take time to reach the roots, settle and normalise the stigma around seeing live-in as an evil of the society.

IS THERE A GENESIS IN HISTORY?

It is not a novice concept and dates back to ancient times. The Vedas of the Vedic Period that mention about the mantras, yajnas and hymns also provide an insight into the Gandharva type of marriage that involves the marriage of a man and a woman that mutually consent and no participation of any of the families, just a word-of- mouth commitment. Hence, the Vedas permitted live-in-relationship; what is now referred to by the western world as cohabitation, living together without the solemnization of marriage, and it always persisted in the society. The above- mentioned speaks about the Hindu mythology and its belief. Looking at the other side of the coin, Adam and Eve were the first non- married couple in the history, they were not aware that an institution of marriage also existed. Their relationship basically depended on their dependency towards each other, with nothing as a ritual, pre- marriage rituals and marriage certificate, they were driven by the Darwinian philosophy of survival of the fittest.

With the advent of the British laws in India, evil practices were banned but it cannot be said with confirmation because they were practiced in hidden way. Hence, the word might be new but it has been seen in the Vedas running through the ancient and the medieval periods and it is not a new concept to India though it is now being practiced on large scale.

WHY IS THERE AN INCREASE IN THE CONCEPT?

Not only the western countries from this concept emerged but also the other countries that were influenced by this trend view cohabitation as an option to live together before marriage to comprehend the compatibility of their relationship. Scandinavian countries have been on the forefront to start this trend, before the mid of 1990s the graph level was stable but after that period the line has been increasing with an upward curve. The couples wish to maintain their single status for financial reasons, in some cases the couples have the notion that there is no need of marriage and it is not a necessity and they hate to be divorced therefore they enter into a live-in-relationship. "For instance, in the European Values Study (EVS) of 2008, the percentage of respondents who agreed with the assertion that "Marriage is an outdated institution" was 37.5% in Luxembourg, 35.4% in France, 34.3% in Belgium, 31.2% in Spain, 30.5% in Austria, 29.2% in Germany, 27.7% in Switzerland, 27.2% in Bulgaria, 27.0% in the Netherlands, 25.0% in Slovenia."

Some have the pretext that living together make them save money as there are high and tight budgets of today's economy that lead them to cooperate with each other. "Researchers suggest that couples live together as a way of trying out marriage to test compatibility with their partners, while still having the option of ending the relationship without legal implications."

<u>INTERNATIONAL PERPECTIVE</u>

Canada has seen an increase in the rates of cohabitation as one of its territories named Quebec has produced children from cohabitating partners and this surge is due to the public rebel against traditional and conservative values as it is socially controlled. The legal issues surrounding this concept is complex but the surge concludes that live-in is exercised by the public at a large scale. In the United States, this concept emerged in the 20th century, "Cohabitation was almost impossible in the United States prior to the 1960s. Laws prevented unmarried couples from registering in hotels and it was very difficult for an unmarried couple to obtain a home mortgage. From 1960 to 1998, cohabitation moved from disreputable and difficult to normal and convenient" Other countries such as the China has shown that premarital cohabitation has become a necessity and decreases the rate of divorce and thus it has gained popularity amongst the young adults. Indonesian states have criminalized the practice of cohabitation and there are always protests upon the inhumane actions of the police. In Britain, there is a conflict over the issue that whether the marriages should be imposed upon people and this has been supported by the Conservative Party or focus should be on parenting rather than a spouse and this has been supported by the Labour Party and the Liberal Democrats; in Russia, the partners are reluctant to cohabit before marriage, a civil marriage registration, afterward the marriage. Switzerland being the epitome for progress has itself been the last to introduce gender equality and has a tradition of strong conscrvatism, adultery got decriminalized and it was in late 20th century that Valais, the last canton ended the prohibition on cohabitation and now the data shows that births outside marriage has increased. European Union is a union of 27 members and the cohabitation has become a commonplace. "The fact that many couples choose to live together without formalizing their relation is also recognized by the European Union. A 2004 directive forbids EU members from denying entry or residence of partners with whom the Union citizen has a durable relationship, duly attested."

INDIAN PERSPECTIVE

In Asian countries, earlier this feature did not exist in the operating system but since now the greater number of individuals are getting educated and independent, the influence and the colours of the western culture has started showing its colour. Looking at Nepal, the acceptance of couples staying together is consented only after the marriage and they do not have any laws to protect the cohabitating partners. Same trend is followed in Bangladesh and China, where the adults now in urban areas are swayed towards the western ideas and cultures.

Speaking of India, it has been considered as a taboo and it is certainly not a dime a dozen because the Hindus and the Muslims stand against it, it can be found in urban areas but not so dominant in rural areas, where the boys and the girls are forced to marry someone and their voices go unheard because of the fear factor, their studies and also early marriage. It goes against the social norm of the society and hence it is highly condemned. The reason for condemnation is mostly the unacceptance as it breaks the norms of the society while few believe that marriages after live-in become a failure.

JUDICIAL INTERPRETATION

Judiciary has been set aside from the definition of State in Article 12 of the Constitution of India and certainly the framers of the longest written Constitution had an eagles' eye that saw judiciary as the protector and guarantor of the people of India, they can approach the court if their fundamental rights are violated. Hence, the judiciary has always come up with its interpretation indifferent to the society's perception and has exercised its power. The institution of marriage has social and legal recognition across society in India. The personal law is based on custom and the new emerging concept of live- in has again called in the judiciary to check upon the prevailing notion.

In the Supreme Court judgement of S. Khushboo V. Kanniammal, the apex court of India held that "there is no statutory offence that takes place when adults willingly engage in sexual relations outside the marital setting, with the exception of `adultery' as defined under Section 497 IPC." In the present case, the court took reference of the previously decided case of Lata Singh V. State of U.P. wherein it was concluded that a girl of major age is free to marry anyone she likes or "live with anyone she likes" and that if two adults' consent to be in live-in relationship, it does not amount to offence.

In S.P.S. Balasubramanyam V. Suruttayan, it was established that if a couple live together posing as husband and wife for a long period of time, it can be clearly presumed that there is legality of marriage between them. In other case of Tulsa & Ors. V. Durghatiya, the court guided the people through the use of Sections 50 and 114 of the Indian Evidence Act, 1872, "it is clear that the act of marriage can be presumed from the common course of natural events and the conduct of parties as they are borne out by the facts of a particular case."

"Where a man and woman are proved to have lived together as man and wife, the law will presume, unless, the contrary be clearly proved that they were living together in consequence of a valid marriage, and not in a state of concubinage."

Another landmark case was that of Indra Sarma V. V.K.V. Sarma that gained limelight throughout the country as the court called for the introduction of a legislation for this so that the women and the children born out of this relationship are protected and the rights be adhered to.

Certain conditions have been put forward by the Supreme Court if a couple needs maintenance in live-in:

"The couples must hold themselves out to society as being akin to spouses.

(b) They must be of legal age to marry.

(c) They must be otherwise qualified to enter into a legal marriage, including being unmarried.

(d) They must have voluntarily cohabited and held themselves out to the world as being akin to spouses for a significant period of time."

Section 16 of the Hindu Marriage Act, 1955 and Section 26 of the Special Marriage Act, 1954 preserve the right of the child born out of the live-in couples, it should be treated indifferently to others but such rights only extend to the property of parents and not as one inherited by the Hindu Undivided Family.

<u>CONCLUSION</u>

The live-in- relationships always had two coins with people in support and against it. The judiciary has always come forward to help those in need by interpreting the prevailing laws and providing protection, hence it fulfils its every duty as the protector of our rights, the stigma around this new concept has to be eradicated and this can only happen when a greater number of people look at the brighter side of the face. With evolution and education ruling our country, the youth of today wants to be independent and hence the legislature should take a stand and enact laws and bring to the podium for people who wish to break the taboo of the society.

<u>Author's Bio</u>

Shriyanshi is a law scholar pursuing her B.A. LLB(H) from Amity University Lucknow Campus. Having completed her schooling from City Montessori School, Lucknow she decided to pursue her career in law which according to her is the only means to eradicate the evils of the society and bring justice to the needy and the innocent. She has keen interest in reading books and writing articles, she has also been the part of National Spell Bee which is conducted almost every year. Being a determined and dedicated worker, she has always done well in her academics too. The success mantra for her is to aim at your goal and not be attracted by the worldly possessions.

CHAPTER THREE

PANDORA'S BOX OF CONSUMER DISPUTE ARBITRATION: REVISITING LEGALITY IN THE DYNAMIC LANDSCAPE

Author: Prateek, B.A.,LL.B from Army Institute of Law, Mohali.

<u>**Introduction**</u>

With the exponential growth of arbitration as an alternative dispute resolution mechanism, Indian Legislature and Judiciary have manifested a seemingly high propensity to rule in favour of this mechanism. Optically, this has been in the form of legislative amendments that streamline the arbitration procedure, such as the amendment to s.34 of the Arbitration and Conciliation Act, 1996 ("A&C Act"). On the judicial end, this manifestation has been in the form of precedents that widen the horizon of arbitrability. This prioritization of arbitration, along with the adoption of principles like that of "Kompetenz-Kompetenz", has paved the way for strengthening mandatory arbitration through enforcement of pre-dispute arbitration agreements.

Mandatory arbitration through standard form contracts is primarily unilateral, with little to no scope for negotiation. Courts have held that once the statutory requirements under s.8 have been satisfied, the court must refer the dispute to arbitration. Yet, this process is not as straightjacket as it may seem, since it has also been established that certain disputes are non-arbitrable by virtue of the dispute's nature.

Such discourse by the Supreme Court resulted in the creation of a new regime with respect to arbitrability of consumer disputes, whereby the court upheld party autonomy by stipulating that consumer may opt into arbitration if so desired, but also provided a safeguarding mechanism by upholding a consumer's right to approach Consumer Courts regardless of the existence of pre-dispute arbitration agreements. Yet, where party autonomy is held to be one of the pillars of arbitration law, this principle of autonomy may be vitiated in the case of certain unequitable relationships and hence there is a need for state intervention under the banner of public policy.

Mandatory Arbitration Agreements in Unequal Contractual Relationships

With this increasing adoption of standard-form contracts in the Business-2-Consumer world, some use-cases of such agreements have created a space for jurisprudential discourse from a safeguarding perspective. This issue largely revolves around contracts finding their genesis in a paradigm of unequal power dynamics between parties to a contract. Manifestation of such unequal power dynamics is usually in the form of unilateral standard form-contracts, harming the claim of party autonomy that arbitration otherwise champions. Two such power-dynamics include the employer-employee relationship, and the business-consumer relationship.

- A Parallel: Employer-Employee Relationships

Prima facie, employer-employee relationships provide a manifestation of unequal relationships in terms of power dynamics. Recognition of this inequality enables state to undertake the drafting of protective labour legislations. In countries like France, Germany and United Kingdom, one can observe this protective perspective manifesting in a limitation on, or even outright refusal to, enforce pre-dispute arbitration agreements with respect to disputes over wrongful dismissal of an employee. Such an approach is relatively absent from US Jurisprudence where not only do courts enforce pre-dispute arbitration, but have also upheld derogation of worker rights like the right to collective action in favour of arbitration clauses excluding class action suits.

Indian perspective on the subject differs to a large extent, and provides an exceptional solution to the discourse on arbitrability of consumer disputes. With respect to arbitrability of labour disputes under the Industrial Disputes Act, 1947, courts have held that these are not arbitrable under the A&C Act. Scheme of the Industrial Disputes Act, 1947 was deeply analysed by the court to conclude that the statute provides for a unique and specialised mechanism for the resolution of labour disputes, and if any dispute was to be adjudicated on outside the courts and tribunals established under the Act, these proceedings must still be governed by the Industrial Disputes Act, 1947. It has also been held that there are compelling reasons evolving from public policy that necessitate the resolution of labour disputes through such a specialised statutory mechanism. Hence, even if arbitration is to be undertaken in consumer disputes, it must be under the mechanisms established by the Industrial Disputes Act itself, and cannot be governed by the A&C Act.

- Mandatory Arbitration Agreements in Consumer Disputes:

Foreign Perspective

Jurisprudential discourse on the subject is ample and widespread in foreign jurisdictions. In terms of susceptibility of the subject of arbitrability to challenges and limitations on the grounds of nature of dispute, stark contrast can be drawn between views followed in US v EU.

United States of America

American law on arbitration has seen immense impact through judicial interpretation of the Federal Arbitration Act, 1925 ("The FAA"). The FAA provides that once the presence of an arbitration clause has been proved, the court is necessitated to refer the dispute to arbitration. While the initial sentiment was to view the Act as a limited legislation governing a narrow range of commercial disputes, the courts later leaned towards an interpretation where any doubts regarding scope of applicability of the arbitration clause on the dispute was resolved through favouring arbitration as the way out. Objection to arbitration under the FAA is largely limited to unconscionability of the arbitration agreement. Such test has been held to be affected on a case-to-case basis, with due regard being given to the oppressive conduct of the parties.

American prioritization of arbitration shows signs of overreaching harms of the application of consent principle when dealing with question of arbitrability. Although the unconscionability mechanism normatively allows courts to undertake interpretations with a protective view, the unfazed prioritization of arbitration by American Courts led to expansion of the Doctrine of Severability in ways that resulted in elimination of various challenges under the ground of unconscionability. And while there has been recognition of the prohibitive effect that costs may have on consumer tendency to bring disputes to arbitration, certain precedents still push the burden of proving this prohibitive nature of arbitration onto the already disgruntled and possibly incapacitated consumer.

European Union

Arguably, the European Union provides for one of the most equitable and fair standards for implementation and execution of mandatory arbitration agreements pertaining to consumer disputes. The law excludes application of arbitration clauses that have not been individually negotiated, thereby guaranteeing meaningful consent. This safeguard becomes evident with the EU Directive deeming pre-dispute arbitral clauses presumptively unfair in B2C Disputes. Where objections inherent to arbitration (like exorbitant costs) would still remain unresolved to a certain extent, the principal justification of express and ensured consent drastically reduces the propensity of companies exploiting consumers through mandatory arbitration agreements.

Indian Perspective

Stand taken by Indian Courts on the subject can be summarised as the "characterisation of pre-dispute arbitration clauses in B2C relationships as non-binding dispute resolution". The Supreme Court, in M/s. Emaar MGF Land Limited v. Aftab Singh, stipulated this position by positing that where arbitrability and party consent must be respected, the same must not be in a straight-jacket formula. The regime thereby established states that a pre-dispute arbitration agreement in any B2C relationship can be the basis for a consumer to undertake arbitration, but the choice of approaching the Consumer Court is not automatically derogated just by the presence of such an agreement. Hence, court granted consumers with agency over choice of forum, albeit a right exercisable within a limited time frame, with initiation of arbitral proceedings placing an embargo on later seeking protection from Consumer Courts. This approach seems to be a middle ground between the American and the European stance to a large extent.

Court also upheld the protective nature of the Consumer Protection Act, 1986 ("CoPRA, 1986") and extrapolated the extraordinary power of consumer forums that overrides provisions for mechanical reference of disputes to arbitration, from such nature. This protective nature has been upheld earlier on the basis of the Act's scheme and language of the Preamble. Application of this interpretation can be made to the new Consumer Protection Act, 2019 ("CoPRA, 2019") as well, owing to the similarity it has with its predecessor in terms of the importance given to protection of consumer rights, made evident through the stark similarities in terms of the Preamble in both Acts.

Among other precedents, Supreme Court in the Emaar MFG Case relied on the principle of arbitrability established under Booz Allen & Hamilton Inc. v. SBI Home Finance Ltd ("Booz Allen Case"), where the court stipulated that, disputes involving adjudication over rights in rem must usually be kept under exclusive jurisdiction of the public court system. Yet an important clarification was made by the court where it was held that such rule is not a rigid or inflexible one, since disputes involving adjudication of subordinate rights arising out of rights in rem would be arbitrable in nature. This widened scope allows disputes arising out of private contractual B2C relationships to be considered arbitrable as well.

Need-Analysis Under the New Consumer Protection Regime

Post judgment in the Emaar MFG case, India's consumer and arbitration jurisprudences have seen major changes. Where the above-mentioned dichotomy poses a contentious trade-off, the same seems to have been made infructuous due to these alterations. This is largely due to the incorporation of party autonomy, state safeguarding through affordable and expeditious public forums, and integration of means for alternative dispute resolution into the legislative structure of consumer protection.

Implications of the Judgment in Vidya Drolia and Ors. v Durga Trading Company on Arbitrability of Consumer Disputes

Indian jurisprudence on arbitrability of disputes witnessed a major addition post the Emaar MFG Case and Booz Allen Case, through the Supreme Court's verdict in the Vidya Drolia Case. The most valuable contribution of this case was in the form of a four-fold test for determining arbitrability which the court laid down. As per this test, a dispute over the following subject matter would be non-arbitrable:

- Subject matter involving determination of rights in rem.
- Having erga omnes effect, whereby central adjudication is deemed necessary over mutual adjudication.

- Is related to sovereign and/or public interest functions of State.
- Subject matter has, expressly or impliedly, been rendered non-arbitrable under a statute.

While the clarification discussed under the Booz Allen Case excludes application of the first test, the other three are seemingly applicable over consumer disputes.

To begin with, the CoPRA, 2019 includes, within the scope of a consumer complaint, allegations of acts having a wider public implication such as unfair or restrictive trade practice, price gauging, or sale of hazardous goods. Adjudication over such complaints must be made without limiting of the scope of investigation through the privity of contract between the complainant and the producer/seller. Conclusive evidence in this regard is the inability of an arbitral tribunal to give effect to certain remedies like recalling of products en masse, something that Consumer Protection Forums under the CoPRA, 2019 are empowered to order.

Furthermore, in Natraj Studios (P) Ltd. v. Navrang Studios, the Court underlined that public policy requires certain kinds of disputes to be determined by special public forums provisioned for by legislative action, and that parties cannot contract out of the same. Recognition of this principle in consonance with the test laid down in the Vidya Drolia Case would create an interpretation of arbitrability in consumer disputes that is answered in the negative. Except, this conundrum was resolved by the court earlier, where the general principle was held to be that disputes capable of being adjudicated upon by a public forum, may also be capable of adjudication by an arbitral tribunal, and hence the test of public fora may be inadequate to oust arbitrability.

Hence, to conclusively understand the issue, there is a need to analyse the nature of public fora through the optics of the new statute which revamped the sphere of consumer dispute resolution.

Implications of the Consumer Protection Act, 2019

There is a further need to revisit the concept of arbitrability of consumer disputes owing to a change in legislative regime covering the subject. As discussed above, the succeeding Act passed in 2019 revamped the state policy on consumer protection to a large extent, and might have even impliedly assailed the reasoning provided in the Emaar MFG Case. A major point of difference between the CoPRA, 1986 and its successor is that the latter can be seen as a legislative attempt to establish a whole system of dispute resolution, as compared to the predecessor, which largely operated as an effective alternative.

Forum jurisdiction for Consumer Disputes

In Union of India v Competition Commission of India, the Delhi High Court undertook discourse on the subject of the validity of CCI's jurisdiction over disputes where parties to the dispute had a pre-existing arbitration agreement. The court upheld CCI's public function by underlining its special focus as a forum which undertakes investigation from a public perspective, rather than a private one. This, in principle, is concurrent with already established precedents whereby certain disputes are not arbitrable due to the nature of inquiry required to be undertaken falls under the exclusive domain for a specialised public forum.

The court's approach is commendable in its understanding of nuanced differences in scope of investigations undertaken by private and public forums. Expansion of this principle to consumer disputes is essential since a similar nuance to scope of investigation is present under CoPRA, 2019. This has been done with a view of empowering bodies that undertake pre-emptive protection of consumer interests, like the Central Consumer Protection Authority. As a general rule under English Jurisprudence, arbitrability may also be determined by ascertaining whether the arbitral tribunal is empowered to grant the remedy required in the specific case. This principle plays an inherent role in the judgment under Union of India v Competition Commission of India whereby nature of adjudication by a forum was deliberated upon.

Confidentiality of arbitration proceedings vis-à-vis class action consumer suit

Striking need for exclusion of arbitration as an alternative means of consumer dispute resolution further becomes necessary with the recent Amendment to the A&C Act, which introduced the concept of mandatory confidentiality. The provision requires confidentiality to be maintained with respect to the arbitral proceedings by all parties who are a member to the proceedings, with the sole exception to the rule being the usage of this information for the purposes of execution of the arbitral award. Implications of this provision are immeasurable in nature when placing it in the context of consumer disputes. It is already noted that arbitral proceedings are preferred due to the proceedings being conducted in private. This is because it will incentivise producers and sellers to induce consumers to undergo arbitration at any cost, if it is over disputes that may have affected multiple unknowing consumers. Where CoPRA, 2019 envisions the protection of consumers as a class, implications of the confidentiality provision will only make information of misdeeds inaccessible to the general public, thereby reducing propensity of consumers to undertake class-actions.

CoPRA, 2019 expressly allows mediation but no mention of arbitration

The principal justification behind arbitration has always been considered as effective and expeditious resolution of disputes. Yet, although the courts have upheld online arbitration agreements, and consequently, the validity of online arbitral proceedings, the impact of this format on cost cannot be considered comparative to the state-provided alternatives which are present already.

This is where the safeguarding nature of dispute resolution mechanisms under the state gain the upper hand. Courts have professed the nature of CoPRA, 1986 to be one that aims to provide better redressal to consumer disputes, through mechanisms which are accessible, cheaper and expeditious. This mechanisation has been drastically revamped to increase effective dispute resolution through the successive Act. Not only does CoPRA, 2019 improve pre-existing Consumer Forums, it also grants legislative recognition to mediation as an alternative mode of consumer dispute resolution, thus increasing party autonomy and providing agency to consumers through creation of scope for determining resolution on terms deemed effective and sufficient by both parties.

This consideration is not just essential for speedy resolution of disputes, and has much wider implications. With the legislative assent to mediation being given expressly under CoPRA, 2019, attention must be paid to the fourth test provided under the Vidya Drolia Case, where the court stipulated that express or implied bar can be placed on arbitrability of a dispute through a statute. Legislative intent to regulate alternate resolution of consumer becomes evident with s.101(2)(r) of CoPRA, 2019 providing Central Government with the power to bar mediation of certain cases. This feature seems to be missing from the Act's predecessor, making the change in legislative intent fairly evident. Exclusion of any provisions regulating arbitration thereafter, sets out the legislature's intent to not include it as an alternative means of consumer dispute resolution.

Need for judicial precedents in Consumer Disputes

Lastly, in the ever-dynamic world of consumer rights jurisprudence, there is a need for the law to maintain a similar pace to ensure effectiveness. Judicial activism through precedent is an especially effective way to ensure the same. Yet, opportunity to exercise judicial activism is undermined when consumer disputes are resolved in alternative forums. Where mediation still provides for consumers to have agency over the final settlement and is thereby justified, arbitration lacks that excuse. Growth of precedents is not possible through arbitration since arbitral tribunals lack the power to set judicial precedents. This justifies the need for public forum intervention, especially in a field which is still developing, and dealing with adjudication of rights for a vulnerable class.

Conclusion

Consumer Contracts are inherently unequal in terms of power-dynamics, and increasing consumerism has only led to the creation of fast-paced business models that burden their customers with unilateral standard-form contracts. Combined with low awareness among the public in India, there is a necessity for state to protect this vulnerable class. The CoPRA, 2019 is a welcome step in that direction, with its strengthening of public forums, as well as space for mediation as an alternative dispute resolution system.

Yet, it is also important to recognise that all consumer disputes are not of a similar nature. Where some, like losses due to sale of damaged goods, are disputes which are usually exclusively private in nature, others like restrictive trade practices have a wider public implication, and hence require involvement of a public forum. The CoPRA, 2019 already envisions a solution to this conundrum through s.101 of the Act, where Central Government has been granted the power to bar certain disputes from being referred to mediation. If the legislative intent is to allow for arbitration in consumer disputes at the consumer's choice, this choice must be restricted on grounds of the nature of dispute, through a similar legislative provision. Necessity for this express action is also paramount due to the principle of quilibet potest renunciare juri pro se introducto, (i.e., anyone may renounce a law introduced for his own benefit) only being applicable in the cases of laws made for securing private benefits, and not provisions that impact larger public interest.

Further, if space is to be made for arbitration, there needs to be statutory regulation of the process to deal with the threats to equity posed by facets inherent to arbitral procedures. Arbitration is inherently and systematically lopsided, and there is a high chance of costs being prohibitive on consumers who may already be lacking awareness and resources to undertake actions against comparatively well-positioned companies. This manifests in the form of a disincentive for consumers to bring forward any action, since costs of the proceedings may outweigh the claims set out. Lack of awareness and unequitable position may also result in imposition of costs under loser-pays clauses, further creating a need for policing of the arbitration procedures. Solution to this could be in the form of regulations been laid down statutorily under the CoPRA, 2019, to ensure that certain ground-rules are complied with. This could include rules governing decisions over the venue of arbitration and cost-sharing metrics for arbitral proceedings.

Lastly, these changes are essential to uphold the vital position held by Consumer Protection Laws as state action to protect a vulnerable class. Legitimacy of the statue consequently relies on its ability to uphold consumer rights efficaciously, and any lapse in the same would be catastrophic to the larger public interest, and would result in the state's public function becoming infructuous to that extent.

If necessity to allow arbitration as an alternative is deemed overwhelmingly important, then the same must be statutorily regulated for preserving the ethos built by the Consumer Rights Movement. Solution to this can be derived out of the approach taken by Indian Courts while dealing with the issue of arbitrability of labour disputes, which upholds the statutory protections granted to the vulnerable class through special statutes.

PARLIAMENTARY PRIVILEGES IN INDIA

Author: Neha Venkatesh, IV year of B.A.,LL.B(Hons.) From School of Law, Christ (deemed to be University), Bangalore.

This paper mainly emphasises the parliamentary privileges that are currently enjoyed by the parliamentarians. In the democratic setup, the constitution provides for certain privileges. The aim of providing the privileges to the parliamentarians allows them to express their opinions, and express the needs of the people they represent and their political stance on certain issues. The parliament establishes its own norms of procedure and maintains its own discipline, among other things, to guarantee that it can execute its obligations and perform its functions independently and freely. Parliamentary privilege, on the other hand, is frequently misconstrued by the general public, who assume that it provides special protection to the parliamentarians making them the 'elites' in the country.

Despite its long history, parliamentary privilege is not fixed or unchangeable. Social life has changed dramatically as a result of contemporary science and technology, which will undoubtedly impact the evolution of parliamentary privilege.

The paper to begin with covers the key features and the origin of parliamentary privilege and its theoretical background comprising of a jurisprudential analysis based on the concept of privileges given by Hofled through his jural correlatives and jural opposites. Rights and Privileges are jural opposites. Here the rights such as the right to freedom of speech and expression will be illustrated as a right and privilege analysis.

After that, the paper will discuss the challenges in the practice of parliamentary privilege, and the growth of privilege, a comparative analysis of parliamentary privileges in India with that of other countries. The paper will extensively compare the parliamentary privilege system of India with the Privilege Model of the United Kingdom, the United States. And in order to understand the same better, a few landmark judgements will be used to critically understand the national and international models.

Parliamentary privilege has a lot of detractors, thus in order to clear up the misunderstandings and strengthen the position of parliamentary privilege in people's minds, it needs to adapt and develop. As they can consequently be arbitrary, obscure, unjust, unlimited discretionary power and the misuse of the same and against the principles of democracy.

Lastly, a few suggestions regarding the enhancement of the privileges to make them more relevant in the present times will be given. According to common belief, immunity does not shield representatives from unlawful and criminal conduct. For example, if a representative at a meeting makes a speech that constitutes a crime, you must pursue their legal duties. This restores the representatives' rights granted by the constitution and the law.

The term "parliamentary privilege" refers to the right to speak freely "The sum of the peculiar rights enjoyed by each House collectively as a constituent part of the High Court of Parliament, and by Members of each House individually, without which they could not discharge their function... Parliamentary privileges are rights that are absolutely necessary for the proper execution of its powers... Individual Members benefit from them since the House cannot accomplish its tasks without the unrestricted use of its Members' services, and each House benefits from them for the protection of its members and the vindication of its own authority and dignity." Members of Parliament may thus claim parliamentary privilege individually or as a whole.

The majority of jurists prefer the word liberty over the term privilege. Despite Hohfeld's choice for the word privilege, these two notions occupy the same structural position in his theory. Privileges are permitted to behave in a certain manner without being held culpable for the damage caused to those who are unable to seek intervention from the authorities. "The plaintiffs have no rights to the extent that the defendants enjoy privileges," Hohfeld stated. There can't be a contradiction between privilege and rights or claims as termed by the jurist. The legal connection reveals that the individual asserting liberty has no entitlement to the activity to which liberty refers. However, this does not rule out the potential of his meddling with the proceedings.

Hohfeld recognized that there are freedoms in legal systems that aren't accompanied by duties put on others to avoid legal action and that there are frequently significant political reasons for this. Legislators are relieved of the responsibility of imposing a duty on others when someone is given legal liberty. A reasonable legislator may take advantage of political issues when determining whether or not to apply the aforementioned principles in a certain situation.

The rights enumerated in Part III of the Indian Constitution, for example, are the 'privileges' referenced by Hohfeld since they stipulate that the state has no power to interfere with the enjoyment of these freedoms.

Therefore, the parliamentary privileges is a privilege and the parliamentarians have the privilege then the others have a no-right against it. And in turn, they do not have a duty pertaining to the same.

Parliamentary privileges in Westminster systems such as Australia, New Zealand, Canada, the United Kingdom, and others are the result of a real political fight in the United Kingdom between the House of Commons and the Crown (and the House of Lords). The adoption of parliamentary privilege legislation and the application of privilege in Australia, as well as other jurisdictions that have adopted the Westminster model, has been heavily impacted by British precedent. The Commonwealth of Australia, most Australian state jurisdictions, Canada, and New Zealand, for example, have included in some form or another copies of Article 9 of the English

Bill of Rights 1689. 'The freedom of expression, debates, or procedures in Parliament, ought not to be impeached or questioned in any court or venue outside of Parliament,' says Article 9.

In the United Kingdom, or materials exchanged among MPs by House order, there is an absolute common law privilege. The Parliamentary Papers Act 1840 extends this to all papers produced under the House's authority, as well as corrected copies. Extracts are also covered by qualified privilege under the Act.

At the start of each new Parliament, the Speaker asserts the Commons' historic and undeniable rights and privileges. Only Erskine May: Parliamentary Practice codifies the privileges, and the House is the only arbiter of its own privileges. The majority of the claims made are no longer valid, however some are still valid:

Firstly, Freedom of expression that is the members speaking in the House are not liable for defamation and in civil issues, freedom from arrest which are technically outdated and The Commons' access to the Crown (through the Speaker); and that the Commons' decisions should be given the most favorable interpretation possible.

The Privileges that aren't specified explicitly are First, the Right of the House to choose its own members, although election petitions are now determined by the ordinary Courts and The House has the authority to govern its own internal processes, both in terms of issues and procedures. Members and "strangers" have the right to be punished for breaches of privilege and contempt; lastly, Right to be unaffected by others although members are no longer immune from all civil actions

On the other hand, Members of the US Congress have the same parliamentary privileges as members of the British Parliament, which means they cannot be punished for whatever they say on the House or Senate floor. They also have the right to be present in Congress: they may spend the remainder of their sentence in prison or jail, but they can attend Congressional sessions, speak on the floor, vote, and so on. These rights are outlined in the Constitution and have historically been relatively uncontroversial in the United States. Courts have typically applied a relatively restricted interpretation to them. When looking at Congress' capacity to punish contempt, there are differences in the practice and approach to privilege in the United States compared to certain other countries. While privilege in the United States is founded on the Westminster model of parliamentary democracy, each state's legislature has evolved its own unique constitutional system. Early American legislators, on the other hand, looked to the English House of Commons and modelled themselves after its precedents and processes. The political climate in which these legislatures developed had a tremendous impact on them, and they developed a strong hostility to the Stuart rulers.

In Anderson v Dunn, a post-independence case, the Supreme Court recognized Congress' right to punish contempts, stating that such power was required to guarantee Congress was "not exposed to every indignity and interruption that rudeness, caprice, or even conspiracy, may mediate against it." While the Supreme Court had already recognized Congress' right to undertake inquiries as "inherent in the legislative process" in earlier decisions.

The Senate and House of Commons, as well as provincial legislative assemblies in Canada, adopt the British parliamentary authority's concept of parliamentary privilege.

The powers, privileges, and immunities of the Senate and the House of Representatives, and of the members and committees of each House, shall be those declared by the Parliament, and until declared, shall be those of the United Kingdom's Commons House of Parliament, and of its members and committees, at the establishment of the Commonwealth.

In 1987, the Commonwealth of Australia's Parliament defined its privileges in order to overturn two Supreme Court of New South Wales decisions that limited parliament's right to freedom of expression. The cases in issue concerned whether witnesses who testified before a parliamentary committee might be cross-examined on such testimony during a criminal prosecution. The Senate contended that such evidence might be used to prove some significant fact, such as that a person testified before a committee at a certain time, but that it could not be used to assist either the prosecution or the defense.

Articles 105 and 194 of the Indian Constitution establish the privileges of parliament and state legislatures, respectively.

Articles 105(3) and 194(3) state categorically that the powers, privileges, and immunities of each House shall be such as may be defined by parliament by law; the provision also states that, until such law is made, the House and its members shall enjoy all the rights that "shall be those of the House of Commons and its members and committees, immediately before the coming into force of section 15 of the Constitution (Forty-fourth Amendment) Act, immediately before the coming into force of section 15

However, a comprehensive codification is required as only those privileges will be codified by the legislature that are acceptable to the executive administration of the day and have a majority in the legislature. Privileges, on the other hand, should not be limited to the governing party or parties, but should apply to all members. The overall effect would be a reduction in privileges.

Codification will crystallize privileges, leaving no room for interpretation of privileges as they now exist in the British Parliament to broaden or amend them. Today, there is a chance to adapt the concepts that underpin privileges in the United Kingdom to Indian situations.

However, in light of the greater public interest and democratic norms, the prospect of a few privileges being curtailed seems to be too weak and fragile to be maintained.

CHAPTER FIVE

HUMOUR : AN ESSENTIAL FOR SURVIVAL

Author : Akanksha, I year of B.A.,LL B from Amity University Jharkhand.

The case starts with the five explorers being trapped in a cave as the entrance was obstructed because of land slide. To save them , rescuc team forwarded their steps but because of another fresh landslide they were not able to reach out there and even ten of them died . Days and nights were passing by like anything . No animal flesh or vegetable was available . It was becoming quite difficult for those five explorers to survive . Suddenly on the twentieth day , one ray of hope entered in their cave , they found out one wireless portable device from which they can send and receive messages and as a result they were able to communicate with the rescue team . Rescue team informed them that at least they need ten more days to pave out the way for those explorers . After that they heard this they thought to connect with the health experts , the health experts suggested that the survival possibility without food is very less for another ten days . After that they did not had any conversation for eight hours , they did not received any messages . They all were in dilemma that what to do next , one men suggested to eat any one of them and this will be decided by the dice mcthod . As the dice was about to cast , one of those five explorers named Roger Whetmore decided to withdraw himself from that game , when other heard his statement , they considered it breach of faith and rolled the dice on behalf of him . Co-incidently the dice went against him and thus as a result he was killed and eaten up by others to satisfy their hunger . After two days that is on the thirty second day , rescue team were able to make out the way and there they found out only four explorers , thus they rescued those four explorers and the four explorers were saved . After they were rescued , the four explorers were provided with medications and treatment . When they recovered after some time they were charged for the murder of that one explorer Roger Whetmore . The bench of judges which were involved in the decision making part were – Chief Justice Truepenny , Justice Foster , Justice Tatting , Justice Keen and Justice Handy . At the time of judgement , the question arised that whether it was correct to snatch the right of protection of life to save life . Bench of five judges sat together to reach out to the conclusion part . Basic Law which was used in this case was that whoever shall wilfully take the life of another shall be given the punishment of death . Chief Justice Truepenny said that murder statute definitely applies here in the defendant's part . Justice Foster used the theory of natural justice . He used the maxim – cessante ratione legis , cessat et ipsa lex which meant that when the reason for law ceases , the law itself ceases . When Roger Whetmore was killed by the other four explorers then the other four explorers were in the state of nature . He also said that , when the ten rescue men lost their lives for the sake of those five explorers so that their life can be saved then why not just one explorer save the lives of other four explorers at the cost of one . Justice Tatting was not able to distinguish between his emotional and intellectual side and thus he withdrew himself from the above case . Justice Keen gave the principle of positivism . He said that as one private citizen stated that if he were the Chief Executive , he would pardon all the men , as they have already suffered a lot earlier only . The question which was in this case was it's not whether what those four explorers did was right or wrong , whether it was wicked or good , instead the main question which arises that whether the defendant within the meaning of the statute wilfully took the life of Roger Whetmore . Lastly , Justice Handy said that this case is based upon Legal Realism – that is common sense . He was only disappointed because none of them raised the question that whether it was unilateral or bilateral and whether Whetmore's withdrawal from the game which was to cast the dice could not be considered as the revoke of the offer prior to the action which was taken . Two judges affirm the conviction while the another two overturn the conviction , the fifth judge didn't reached to the conclusion part and thus he withdrew himself from the above case . Finally , the result came as that they will be spend their life in imprisonment for six months and after that they will be hanged on the charge of murder of that one explorer named Roger Whetmore .

We could say that the case of Speluncean Explorers is quite full of tragedy and ups and downs. Thereby reaching towards the conclusion part we can assume that possibility of being rescued of all the five explorers might had been the best one if the rescue operation had been done quite more accurately and if on the day of communication with the explorers they didn't gave them the deadline of ten days as after two days only they were rescued and even the explorers could have had more patience .

CHAPTER SIX

SUFFERING DURING THE LOCKDOWN, DOMESTIC VIOLENCE AND WOMEN'S SAFETY

Author: Vaibhav Gupta, IV year of B.B.A.,LL.B(Hons.) From Himachal Pradesh National Law University, Shimla.

Co-author: Tanisha Gangwal, B.Com.,LL.B(Hons.) From Institute Of Law, Nirma University, Ahmedabad.

INTRODUCTION

Although home is considered to be the safest place for most but this can be disregarded for some. Where in the mist of the pandemic where everyone was asked to be in their home for safety, but controversially not everyone was safe in their houses, there was this lurking evil in the society called domestic violence which does not see whether that human is of which caste, creed, age or gender the abuser abuse the victim without any boundation.

There was a rise in the cases of domestic violence due to the lockdown caused by the pandemic as it was already prevalent in the society but got fuelled by the mandatory guidelines to stay at home, social distancing, economic uncertainties and anxiety.

While there is a possibility that both men and women can be victims of domestic violence, while women are most likely to be a victim of such evil. As in India the mentality of the society is very patriarchal, this creates higher chances for women to fall in this vicious trap.

Women safety has been on higher risk during this lockdown as the data was collected by the National Commission of Women raised an alert just after the lockdown started in India. This very well depicts and clears us of the doubt that women were at a very higher risk during the midst of lockdown.

<u>WHAT IS DOMESTIC VIOLENCE?</u>

Domestic violence is not slaved to circumstantial needs; it is a virus prevalent in the mind of the abuser which always does not need triggering. "Domestic abuse, also called "intimate partner violence" or "domestic violence", can be defined as a pattern of behavior in any relationship that is used to obtain or retain power and control over an intimate partner."

Abuse can be in any way i.e. it can be either in a physical way i.e. battery or grievous hurt, in manner of sexual abuse, emotional by defaming or disrespecting the person's consciousness, economic by depriving the person of its basic needs or psychological actions or threats of actions that influence another person.

"Domestic abuse is not a predicament to any bias it can happen to anyone of any race, sexual orientation, religion, age, or gender. It can occur within a range of relationships including couples who are married, living together or dating. Domestic violence affects people of all socioeconomic backgrounds and education levels."

Therein domestic violence is a very prevalent curse on the society which is usually on women and it got triggered by the lockdown which forced everyone to stay at home and increased cases on the crime.

<u>DOMESTIC VIOLENCE AGAINST WOMEN</u>

According to Section 3 of The Protection of Women Against Domestic Violence Act, 2005-

"Definition of domestic violence.—For the purposes of this Act, any act, omission or commission or conduct of the respondent shall constitute domestic violence in case it—

(a) harms or injures or endangers the health, safety, life, limb or well-being, whether mental or physical, of the aggrieved person or tends to do so and includes causing physical abuse, sexual abuse, verbal and emotional abuse and economic abuse; or

(b) harasses, harms, injures or endangers the aggrieved person with a view to coerce her or any other person related to her to meet any unlawful demand for any dowry or other property or valuable security; or

(c) has the effect of threatening the aggrieved person or any person related to her by any conduct mentioned in clause (a) or clause (b); or

(d) otherwise injures or causes harm, whether physical or mental, to the aggrieved person. Explanation I.—For the purposes of this section,—

(i) "physical abuse" means any act or conduct which is of such a nature as to cause bodily pain, harm, or danger to life, limb, or health or impair the health or development of the aggrieved person and includes assault, criminal intimidation and criminal force;

(ii) "sexual abuse" includes any conduct of a sexual nature that abuses, humiliates, degrades or otherwise violates the dignity of woman;

(iii) "verbal and emotional abuse"

(iv) "economic abuse"

As mentioned above domestic violence on women is not just in a physical way, it goes beyond those restricted parameters.

One out of three women has suffered domestic violence whether in a physical way or in a sexual way. "During the first four phases of the COVID-19-related lockdown, Indian women filed more domestic violence complaints than recorded in a similar period in the last 10 years. But even this unusual spurt is only the tip of the iceberg as 86% women who experience domestic violence do not seek help in India. In 2020, between March 25 and May 31, 1,477 complaints of domestic violence were made by women. This 68-day period recorded more complaints than those received between March and May in the previous 10 years."

The reasons of domestic violence

Patriarchy: In India some people have very traditional beliefs and they think that they have the right to control their partner/spouse, and that women aren't equal to men.

"According to NFHS data, 42% of the surveyed men think there is at least one valid reason for wife-beating."

Societal influence: Some abusers learn violent behavior from their own family, people in their community/society or other cultural influences as they grow up.

Boys who learn that women are not to be respected or valued and who see violence directed against women are more likely to abuse women when they grow up or get married.

Girls who witness domestic violence in their families of origin are more likely to be victimized by their own husbands because what they are witnessing from childhood created a fear in them.

Economic causes: Unemployment, consumption of alcohol and drugs may also contribute to violent behavior of men.

Socio-Cultural: Honour killings and Dowry related deaths are also a reality that testifies domestic violence.

Individual Factor: Some abusers may feel this need to control their partner because of extreme jealousy, low self-esteem, difficulties in regulating anger and other strong emotions, or when they feel inferior to the other partner in education or socioeconomic background which again leads to the domestic violence.

LOCKDOWN AND DOMESTIC VIOLENCE

Just after few days of the lockdown started in India, the National Commission of Women (NCW) noted a rise in the number of domestic violence complaints received via email. The NCW chairperson was of a belief that the original figure is likely to be higher, since the bulk of complaints come from women who send their complaints by post, and might not be able to use the internet.

Between the beginning of March and April 5th, the NCW received 310 grievances of domestic violence and 885 complaints for other forms of violence against women, many of which are domestic in nature—such as bigamy, polygamy, dowry deaths, and harassment for dowry.

The number of cases reported are most likely not proportional to the actual rise in domestic violence. As the victims being locked in with their abusers may not be able to get access to a mobile phone, nor the space and time to call for help. Most avenues to seek help or to physically remove themselves from their situations are impaired.

Being trapped in a space with violent or manipulative individuals could lead to increased rates and intensity of threats, physical, sexual, and psychological abuse, humiliation, intimidation, and controlling behaviour. The ability to isolate a person from family and friends, monitor their movements, and restrict access to financial resources, employment opportunities, education, or medical care is heightened by a lockdown. These behaviours often have lasting effects on people, and can significantly affect mental health and well-being.

"Invisible Scars, an NGO working on an initiative to help domestic violence victims, has also seen a rise in complaints. In cases of physical domestic violence, depending upon the severity of the abuse, they guide the victims how to go about registering a complaint with the police. Its founder says they encourage victims to speak to someone if they are hesitant to approach the police. This is done after understanding the details of the abuse, both past and present.

"Since the victim most likely lives with the abuser and is stuck with him 24/7 at this point, we have to be very careful. For one of our victims, we suggested asking her to get a written undertaking from her husband and in-laws that they won't isolate her from her family and will not beat her," she says.

Coronavirus has exposed us to our dependence on house help. Most families don't have live-in help and with the lockdown part-timers are unavailable. Says Varkha Chulani, clinical psychologist and psychotherapist at Mumbai's Lilavati Hospital: "Not used to getting their hands dirty, many men are struggling to cope. They feel they are being bossed around, to do the dishes, wash their clothes. Their ego is getting bruised as men are unable to stand being told to help. Stereotypical ideologies exist - it's the woman's job to cook, clean, wash. It's the man's job to earn. So even though we seem to have progressed in paying lip service to be 'liberal', the true test is in the living. And this confinement is throwing up the 'real' mindsets of partners."

'Mpower 1 on 1' is a newly launched helpline in Mumbai to report domestic abuse and help the victim. They got a call this Sunday from a woman who was sounding anxious and breaking into sobs. She had a fight with her husband on some petty issues. It soon escalated and her husband beat her up badly. Feeling helpless and vulnerable, she couldn't go out because of the lockdown. Dr. Ambrish Dharmadhikari, psychiatrist and head of medical services at Mpower says his team counselled her on the phone and asked her to report to the police. "But the sad part is, now the police are busy enforcing the lockdown to curb the spread of Coronavirus," says Dharmadhikari.

The violence of domestic abuse is worse in the poorer section of the society. Psychologist Padma Rewari says her own domestic help has an abusive, alcoholic husband. Now going without alcohol and cooped up in a small room, he has got more violent. For victims like her, there are NGOs like Stree Mukti Sanghatan for help. "The women should approach free counseling and use the online facility for reporting the crime," says Rewari. "The victims of physical abuse may find it helpful to have a safety plan in case the violence escalates. This includes having a neighbor, friend or relative or shelter identified to go to in the event they need to leave the house immediately for safety," she adds. As the lockdown and limited movement outside the house appears to be a long drawn affair, the best recourse for victims of physical abuse is to report the crime and seek help.

This grievous increase in was larger in the backward section of the society as due to lockdown people were deprived from their source of income and many were also deprived of their basic necessities as they are habitual of being the bread earner of the house which leads to aggression and frustration in the abuser as they were not able to vent it out anywhere this raised the number of cases of domestic violence, as India being a patriarchal society women were highly prone to the consequences of men's frustration as in the society women are considered to be very weak and looked down.

<u>CONCLUSION</u>

Domestic violence is a very living evil which is day by day eating the society. The victims lay off to the hands of such an evil is sadly women of our society can also be termed as the most fragile section of the society. The spread of the novel coronavirus has created a pyramid of problems for the people to even cope with it. Due to lack of cure and treatment to this disease people are forced to stay in their houses and be deprived of the help they need. As the only solution at present is the lockdown to be prevailed in the society. However, this has resulted in a paradox of social distancing, which includes issues such as economic instability, mental health problems, and isolation.

Although there have been researches exploring the impact of COVID-19, there is a lack of rigorous literature highlighting these issues from the perspective of gender. This also involves the issue of rising gender violence during the pandemic. COVID-19 has not only led to an increase in the cases of gender-based violence but has disconnected them from their support networks. To reduce the prevalence of the issue, it is crucial to acknowledge the extent of gender-based violence, reimaging government policies, and support networks to make it easier for the victims to access them and, lastly, create awareness about the issue as well as the resources available to tackle it.

K.M.NANAVATI V. THE STATE OF MAHARASHTRA

Author: M.Faizunisha, V year of B.A.,LL.B. from Government Law College Vellore

Introduction

In the history of the Indian JudiciaryK.M.Nanavati v. The state of Maharashtra case is one of the landmark Judgements. This case was about a naval officer Kawas Manekshaw Nanavati, who was accused under section 302 for the murder of Prem Ahuja, his wife's paramour. An unprecedented media coverage was received by this case. The K.M.Nanavati case is also widely recognized as the last case to be heard as a Jury trial in India. As a result of this case the Government abolished the jury system. This case highlights important legal points such as grave and sudden provocation, the burden of proof and the plea of general exemption. The article analyzes the gripping details of this case. Facts of the case 1. The petitioner K.M.Nanavati was second in command of the Indian naval ship "Mysore". Due to the nature of his service, he shifted to Bombay with his wife Sylvia and their three children. 2. In Bombay they met through Agniks, a common friend of Nanawati and a Businessman named Prem Bhagwan Ahuja and his sister Mamie Ahuja. 3. As a part of his service Nanavati had to go frequently away from bombay for long durations leaving his wife and children behind. 4. In his absence, Sylvia and Prem Ahuja became close friends; they often spent time together later Ahuja became Sylvia's paramour. 5. When Nanavati returned from his ship after April 18, 1959. He tried to be affectionate to his wife on multiple occasions but she was not being responsive. 6. On 27 April 1959, Nanavati came to know about the illicit relationship his wife had. when he asked her whether she is faithful to him she indicatedhim by shaking her head as no. 7. In the heat of agony, Nanavati went to his ship and acquired a stacked pistol and then went to Prem Ahuja's office. 8. After discovering that he was not in the office, at that point he then headed to Ahuja's residence and shot him dead. 9. He then surrendered himself in the police station. 10. The jury with an 8 : 1 verdict declared K.M.Nanavati, the accused, not guilty under section 302. 11. However the Sessions Judge disagreed with the decision of the jury, the learned Sessions Judge submitted the case under Section 307 of the Code of Criminal Procedure, 1973 to the Bombay High court.

12. The Hon'bleHigh Court enumeratedthe accused guilty under section 302 of the IndianPenal Code, 1860. 13. Then throughthe SLP, an appeal was made to the Hon'bleSupreme Court , also an application was made to the governor under Article 161. Judgement Analysis The judgment evolved mainly around two issues and the first one was that of the sessions court referringthe matter to the Higher Court owing to the judge's disagreement with the decisionof the jury.

Evidence was also proved in the form of letters written by Slyvia to Ahuja and Extra Judicial Confessions were taken into account. The jury however, reached the decision of him being found not guilty by majority of 8:1. This became the reason for the Sessions Judge for referring the case to the Hon'ble High Court of Bombay under Section 307 of the Code of

Criminal Procedure, 1893.

Section 307: If in any such case the Judge disagrees with the verdict of the jurors or of a majority of jurors on which any accused person had been tried is clearly of opinion that it is necessary for the ends of justice to submit the case in respect of such accused person to the High Court. He shall submit the case accordingly recording the grounds of his opinion and when the verdict is one of acquittal stating the offence which he considered to have been committed and in such case if the accusedis further chargedunder the provisions such charge as if such verdict had been one of conviction.

On appeal to the High Court, it was contended on behalf of the appellant that under Section 307 of the Code of Criminal Procedure it was incumbent on the High Court to decide the competency of the reference on a perusal of the order of reference by Hon'ble Sessions Court. The fact that it had no jurisdiction to go into the evidence for the purpose that Hon'ble High Court was not empowered by Section 307(3) of the Code to set aside the verdict of the jury on the ground that the jury was wrong and that the verdict was perverse.

It was finally held that the contentions were without substance and the appeal must fail. The words "for the ends of justice" in section 307 indicate that the Judge disagreeing with the verdict must be of the opinion that the verdict was one which no reasonable body of men could reach on the evidence, coupled with the words clearly of the opinion gave the Judge a wide and comprehensive discretion to suit different situations.

Therefore, the Judge disagreed with the verdict and recorded the grounds of his opinion the referencewas competent, irrespective of the questionwhether the Judge was right in differing from the jury or forming such an opinion as to the verdict. There is nothing in Section 307(1) of the Code that lends support to the contention that though the Judge had complied with the necessaryconditions the High Court should reject the reference without going into the evidenceif the reasons given in the order of reference did not sustain the view expressed by the Judge.

Another issue before the appellate court was that of mens rea involved. Where the prosecution said that it was a planned murder, the defense went to contend that it was in the heat of the moment and that two shots went to hit the deceased while both the parties entered into a grave brawl. While the former was contending that the accusedshould be punished under Section 302 of the IndianPenal Code, the latter based its argumentson the exception of grave and sudden provocation as provided in section 300 of the Indian Penal Code.

The prosecution established mens rea by proving that the act of going to the Navy ship, procuring a gun and six cartridges and carrying them all in a brown envelope clearly indicate his intensionto conceal the fact that he was going to murder someone. In addition to this, the accused surrendering himself to the police indicates that he had planned to kill the deceased.

On the other hand, the defense has put forth its contention saying that on getting to know the relationship between his wife and Ahuja, the accusedwent to give him a proposal of marrying his wife to which he got an answer "Do I have to marry every woman that I sleep with" This reply of his, according to defense heated up an argument between two and subsequently the accused shot him in sudden provocation in the heat of the moment. Relying on the principle of presumption that accusedis innocent until proven guilty, the higher judiciary went through thorough examination of the witnesses as per the provisions of the Evidence Act and Code of Criminal Procedure.

Both the parties were given equal and sufficient chance with the Burden of Proof primarily being on the prosecution. In the light of contentions raised, arguments advanced and evidence adduced, On 24 November 1961, the Supreme Court upheld the conviction granted by the High Court and sentenced Nanavati to life imprisonment for culpable homicideamounting to murder.

<u>Conclusion</u>

The landmark judgment was able to grab the attention of the nation and media owing to the fact that the crime of adultery had given a birth to the crime of murder not amounting to culpablehomicide. The accused moreover was a decoratedofficer of IndianNavy and such crime committed by him got accepted by the society owing to the pitiful journalism towards him. The burden of proof upon the prosecution was released by establishing the facts to utmost claritywhich is indeed an essential in the process of adjudication.

Also, referring the case to higher judiciary and jury being incorrect on point of law was something that pointed out amount of corruption in judiciary resultant of which was abolition of jury system in succeeding Criminal procedure. The Supreme Court has thus once again shown that no one is above the law.

<u>Author's Bio</u>

I'm M.Faizunisha, Final year student of B.A.L.L.B from Government Law College vellore. Right is right even if everyone is against it and wrong is wrong even if everyone is for it, is the lines I truly believe. I wish to become an eminent lawyer and serve justice to everyone.

• 42 •

CHAPTER EIGHT

DOMESTIC VIOLENCE AGAINST WOMEN

Author: Vanshika Sanjay Agrawal, II year of B.B.A.,LL.B. from Symbiosis International University

ABSTRACT

It has been apparent over the past few years domestic violence has been a great issue. It has now become a serious issue since lockdown as It has been observed that during lockdown all the members of the society were seen at home which made a sudden increase to domesticviolence cases. The women who has been a core of a family and a society, the one who gives birth to the child nurtures their life carriesa child for a period of 9monthsin her womb faces their family society shapes an individual strength them, follows culture generation to generation and the biggest thriller is the greatest injustice is done to women. Almost in India every house is facing this issue whether daughter, wife, daughter in-law are being abused physically, mentally, verbally or emotionally. Men and women in India have the same basic rights but women are always discriminated against due to which they get used to it and do not have the freedom and become the victims of domestic violence. So basically this paper draws attention towards domestic violence its causes, types of violence, recommendations, acts for the prevention of domestic violence, consequences, during pandemic.

<u>INTRODUCTION</u>

The most prevalent form of violence globally of women is domestic violence. It is as old as recorded history which is reported basicallyin every society.It has become a seriousissue of public health concern in every community. Discrimination and prolonged cruel based on physical, mental,emotional has been a sociallyaccepted form of every patriarchal society.

Domestic violence has gaineda severe attention of the healthsector because of the detrimental and negative effect on mental, physical health of a female. The two major elements that are combined together are expecting a woman to be an ideal so- called 'role model' and secondly male dominance and consideration of women to be their own property and object belonging to them. Men wanted women to be their puppet and work according to them and not according to their whims and fancies. Violence is not often restricted to husbands, but may extend to boyfriends or other family members who may include parents, siblings or in-laws. Domestic violence is highly prevalent but women try to hide it and keep it confidential. Particularly being torched, beaten or any physicalharm is very commonly seen in many Indian homes.

Domestic violence is definedas behavior in any of the relationship which is used to gain power and control over an intimatepartner. Domestic violenceoccurs when an intimate partneror the family member tries to harm or dominate physically or psychologically to other. It occurs in all religions, culture, race ethnicities can be a predators of domestic violence. Violence against women in particular, sexualviolence are the major concernsand violation of woman's right. In the year 2021, over "2300" domesticviolence complaints were filed betweenJanuary and May with the National Commission for women.

MEANING OF DOMESTIC

Domestic is defined as running of a familyrelation or a house. MEANING OF VIOLENCE Violence is defined as any behaviorinvolving physical forceintended to causea harm or any damage or injuryto a person or property. Oxford dictionary states: "Violence as behavior involving physical force intendedto hurt, kill or damagesomeone or something." WHO defines Violence: "the intentional use of physical force or power, threatened or actual,against another person,oneself, or againsta group, which either resultsin or has a high likelihood of resulting in injury, psychological harm, death and deprivation". Domestic violence means an aggressive or violent behavior within the home that typically involves the violent abuse of an intimate partner or of a spouse. It is the violence that occurs in a domestic setting cohabitation or marriage. It happens behind closed doors and women often definewho has been a victimof violence. Domestic violence against women means act of violence that results in physical, sexual or psychological harm to women, including coercion, acts, arbitrary deprivation of liberty, whetheroccurring in privateor public life.

CAUSES OF DOMESTIC VIOLENCE

There is no single factor for the cause of violence perpetrated against women. It is an amalgamation of historical, religious, cultural and sociological factors that lead to domesticviolence. Following are the causeslaid herewith:

• Historical Factors: Historical factors can be tracked back as superiority complexand a history of the inherent evil of patriarchy society that has prevailed for centuries among men. This form of practice has being followed since past years.

• Religious Factors: This is an another factor which is the root cause of a domestic violence as this can affect to any person who practices any religion, multiple religion, or religion or who engages in any spiritual practices. Abusers may employ religious texts and try to harm.

• Cultural Factors: It usually meansto desire only for a male child over female.All the backward class societies prefer a male as they think that male can do everything for their livelihood whereas female children are born with the mindset of just running the family, doing household work as the family thinks it a waste of money towards a female education. They henceforth do not seek an attention to females althoughbeing aware of the fact that any child is born by a female.

• Sociological Factors: The sociological or the behavioral factor includes factors such as dominating status, anger issues, aggressive attitude, economic hardships, depression, stress, difference in status among others. These are some of the factors for the root cause of domestic violence as due to any anger or stress a man comes home with the same mindset and lashes out at a woman. Neglect of responsibilities due to lack of trust or any other extra marital affairs also leads to domesticviolence.

TYPES OF DOMESTIC VIOLENCE

• Physical Abuse: Physical form is one of the very prominent form of domestic violence against women which involvesa physical or visible touch to a women. It has been defined in the act of domestic violence wherein it includes any act that causes bodily injury or danger to life, development of the victim. Criminal force, criminal intimidation and assault are forms of physical abuse. Some more forms are listed as below: 1. Threatened to hurt with a weapon.

2. Thrown object, hit or pushedyou.

3. Driven recklessly or forced you off the road.

4. Slapped or chokedyou.

5. Beaten or kicked you.

•Sexual Abuse: Sexual abuse is any abuse of a sexual nature which humiliates, abuses or degrades the dignity of a woman. This is done sexually for the mean purpose of derivingpleasure or to harm the reputation of a women. Sexual abuse women is the nature of reproductive coercion. Abusing partner after having sex and causing harm to a sexual part is again considered as sexual abuse.

Sexual abuses includes:

1. Raping a women.

2. Unwillingly without a consent having sex.

3. Forced sex when sick or after a physical abuse.

4. Criticizing sexually.

•Economic Abuse: Economic abuse is the method of threatening to deprive the victim and children of the family from the use of financial assets. Abusers may exploit and sabotage the victim's access to one's own financial assets. This abuse includes acts such as denial of food shelter and basic needs, denial of funds, controlling access to health care and refusal for contribution of funds financially.

•Emotional/Verbal Abuse: This abuse includes threats or remarks made during a domestic relation againstwomen. Empting victim'sself-esteem, humiliating, disrespecting and insulting are the forms of emotional or verbal abuse. Combination of emotional and verbal abuse leads to a psychological abuse. Threats of taking away children is also an emotional abuse. In short,threatening the victimto take away her most valuable thing away from her leads to an emotionalabuse. Criticizing, shoutingloud, manipulating are again some of the emotional abuse that is caused. All the aboveforms of abusesmake-up to the domestic violenceagainst women in India.

DOMESTIC VIOLENCE LAWS IN INDIA

There are two laws in Indiathat deals with the protection of women againstdomestic violence:

DOMESTIC VIOLENCE ACT, 2005

The protection of women from domestic violence act is a civil law that provides protection to a woman from men in a household. This law is not just applicable to the married women; rather, it is applicable in living relationships, as well as the family members includingmothers, daughters, etc. Under this law, women can seek protection of their right to live, violence, financial issues, and maintenance if living apart. It tries to cover a woman who has been in a relationship with an abuser where both the parties have lived together, has shared households and related to marriage, or adoption or relationship in the nature of marriage, family members living jointly are also included. This is an act of the parliament enacted to protect women from domestic abuse. "It was brought into force on 26 October 2006 by the Indian government and Ministry of Women and Child development. The act provide the definition of domestic violence for the first time and thus not include just the physical abuse rather covers emotional, sexual abuse as well. This act provides the appointment of the NGO's and protection officers in order to provide help to the women with respect to medical assistance, legal aid, safe asylum etc. Women are given the right to seek protection against domestic violence. If the women are evicted from the matrimonial households, she is liable and has the right to seek compensation, free legal aid and medical assistance as well as safe shelter. The section 3 of the act includes threat to life, health safety, etc. Harassment of any form of injuries to the aggrieved party by unlawfully demanding any security or dowry or by way of coercing her. This also includes causing harm or injury through mental or physical assault to the aggrieved party.

The aggrieved party includes any women who has been in a domestic violence and is subjected to it by the responded.1 The purpose of this act is to achieve the following goals:

1. To implementsufficient programs for the survivorof domestic violenceand to ensure a recoveryof the health and a normal life of a victim.

2. To ensureproper protection to a victimwhere the act has occurred.

3. To serve the justiceto a victim in any circumstances cost effectively and efficiently and in a convenient manner.

4. To take all the measures to stop the abuser from committing the violence and support them in the rehabilitation center.

5. To complywith the international standards for the protection of domestic abuseand to enforce and apply relevant principles of justice in accordance with such standards.

Section 498A of the Indian Penal Code

1 The Protection of Women from Domestic violence Act, 2005

Domestic violence section 498A of the Indian penal code coversthe cruelty of a husbandor the husband's families towards the married women. Cruelty in this sense refers to any kind a misconduct or misbehave that causes a severe impact on women's life or her health including mental health or causing a suicidal attempt. It also includes the harassment of the women in terms of the dowry by the family members or the husband. Act of cruelty is not limited to the extent rather includes

• Giving punishment to her by locking insidethe room or outside the house.

• Demanding sexual touch in compensation or bad behavioragainst woman's will.

• Mental torture.

• Physical touch or abuse.

• Not providing sufficient food for their survival.

• Denying basic requirements

This section gives the right to lodge a complaint to the members or the relatives of the women against the abuser. This section is particular and important when a woman is scared to complain or open up about her abuse to others for herself. This law states that if convicted under this law the husband or the family members of the husbandare levied a high fine and the imprisonment up to threeyears.

2 EFFECT OF DOMESTIC VIOLENCE DURING COVID 19

There is preliminary evidence that domestic violence cases have increased globally during the pandemic. The restriction imposed to curb the spread of corona virus made a suddenincrease in violence. Everyone was locked at their home due to the pandemic which made a man to frustrate their anger solely upon women which is also the main reason for a sudden rise in domestic violence cases. There was a rise in other violence as well. According to the Ethiopian study it found that almost one in five women faced domestic violence during Covid-19 pandemic. It was also discovered that the homemakers tied in an arranged marriage were at a higher stake of experiencing violence rather than housewives in a love marriage. The domestic violence cases in the first week saw a high rise and the count went on increasing. Extended social distancing and the lockdown imposed for the curb of pandemic led women more vulnerable to domestic violence cases. Women were fighting the shadow pandemic inside the four walls of their house. Tamil Nadu Police received an increase to the number of cases where they received approximately 26 calls and at least 42 such cases every day during the pandemic period. "Similarly, Bangalore police reported a spike in the complaints from 10 calls to 25 calls every day from the victimsof domestic violence". Thus, this indicatesthat the data stated above,the cases of domestic violence were at a larger number during the course of the Country wide lockdown." The National commission for women registered an increase of 94% in complaint cases where women were assaulted in their house during the lockdown". Therefore considering all the facts and circumstances it's been seen that nearly half a billion of women in India are at a higher stake. As covid-19lockdown caused people to spend their more time in their house, more women were assaulted as to early morning markets and were subjected to more of a sexual and verbal harassment while waiting in a water queue. 2 The Protection of women Section 498A of the IPC

Here are some data of the unfortunate realities:

•Cases of domestic violenceduring Covid-19 rose to about"53%" in the first week of lockdown.

•"86% women in Indiahave experienced violencenever seek help while 77% women have not mentionedthe incidents to anyone".

•"31.1% women aged 15-49 years had experienced at least one in their lives the spousal violence".

<u>**RECOMMENDATIONS ON DOMESTIC VIOLENCE**</u>

• Extensive and comprehensive premarital counselling should be providedto a couple as to how to manage their life and their maritalrelationship.

•Women who discloses their physical or sexual abuse done by the intimate partner should be offered a support. Healthcare workers shouldbe the first line off to offeran immediate help.

• Religious leaders should strenuously spreadand make people aware of the domesticviolence in theirplace of worship.

•Youths should be encouraged and must be taught to not behave and detesttowards the women or theirwives.

•There should be public enlightenment and various camps and throughmass communication on the cons of domesticviolence.

•Women opening up and tellingtheir grievances should be supportedand immediate remedyshould be takenas to set an exampleof harassment done to a woman.

• Punishment given to the husbandgrievously should be publicized, so that can be serve as a dissuading to others.

•There should be psychotherapists and counselors to the victim to provide them with proper assistance and help her to overcomethis issue. Government should issue a straight rule for the victims of domestic violence. Women must be made awareof their rightsand some of the basic provisions.

CONCLUSION

Domestic violence is one of the very vulnerable abuses which women are facing. Domestic violence is something which is not seen and is like a parcel of her life. Having looked at this sensitive topic there is a need for raising up the topic for the discussion and bringing it to the notice. Women are also part of a family. she is just not born with this violence against her and running of her family. As we know that, many of the women are illiterate and are from a backward class of the society. They should be made aware of their rights and the basic provisions of law, and should be motivated to take their stand and to lodge a complaint against the abuser. The various causes for the spark of domestic violence within the four walls of the society should be considered and a wise study of the factors involved during violence may prevent various sections of the society from the menace of the domestic violence. Domestic violence has much wider meaning and the relevance but than what is being said in the research paper. In our society which is male dominated and traditionally bounded still treat women as secondarysex which than make her to silentlysuffer the violence.Women in our community are often ignored and neglected. In order to eliminate this horrendous abuse, all must take a stand and make tougher laws for the protection of the victims of the abuse. There is an urgent need for analyzing the factors provoking a particular form of domestic violence. Once these factors are controlled then there could be more number of the victims that could be saved from many other forms of domestic violence to women and our society and India would become a better place to live in. From my study of a research it can be concluded that my theology on domestic violence is proved correct to a greater extent. It would be really appreciable if this act of domestic violence is stopped and may seek an importance to a families to some extent. It's my sincere request to the nation to stop this violence and help women in any of the possible ways.

CHAPTER NINE

FINANCIAL CRISIS AND SYSTEMIC RISK

Author: Chahat Kanchan, II Year of B.A.,LL.B from Kirit P Mehta School of Law, Mumbai.

ABSTRACT

A financial crisis is a disturbance to financial markets in which adverse selection and moral hazard problems worsen to the point where financial markets are unable to properly direct funds to those with the best investment possibilities.

In the present times, financial crises have become somewhat common. This is because the crisis of one country affects the countries around it. The most recent instance is of the Ukraine crisis, which is affecting the countries around it and the countries that are involved in trade with it. But no matter how common they become, they nevertheless result in loss of the economies for the country and its people and the businesses and trade of the country.

KEY WORDS

Financial crisis, Systemic risks, Economy, Great Depression of 1929.

INTRODUCTION

The world has seen numerous financial crises in the past decades. All these events were faced with shocks from people all over the world, for no one foresaw them and hence no one was ready to face them. For instance,

- The worst financial crisis of the 20th century was the Great Depression of 1929, which almost lasted for about a decade. It resulted in what every crisis results, increased unemployment rates and massive loss of income.
- The OPEC Oil crisis of the 1980s, where there was a sudden rise in the price of oil. It resulted in an increase in the level of uncertainty, in the

midst of the outbreak of the Iran-Iraq War (1980-1988).

- The economic downturn of the Japanese economy in the 1990s. in the 1990s, the Japanese economy suffered a prolonged recession, which finally ended in 2002.
- The Asian Financial Crisis of 1997, which began as a currency crisis in Bangkok, and spread to neighbouring economies soon.
- The Financial Crisis of 2007-2008, the only crisis that was worse than the Great Depression of 1929. It caused havoc in the financial markets of the world.
- The contraction of the economy of Ukraine this year due to Russian invasion has sent the country's economy into recession, which is affecting economies in Europe and Central Asia, such as India and United States.

All of these crises were caused because of different events and impacted different countries but all of them had one thing in common, all of them had the same impact. They resulted in falling back of the economy, increase in the unemployment rates, hike in the prices of goods and commodities.

REVIEW OF LITERATURE

D. Besar, P. Booth, KK Chan and J. Pickles, of the Institute and Faculty of Actuaries talk about financial crisis and systemic risks in their paper, Systemic Risks in Financial Services. They talk about the impact of financial crises on the economy of a country and how financial deregulation has played a role in the occurrence of the crises.

Nicole Tham Ping says that the relationship that exists between the fall of assets, the increase in the unemployment rate and a rise in the level of debts are all associated with and are impacts of global financial crises.

K G Viswanathan tells how all the global crises that have occurred in the past till date, have almost the same impact, such as fall in the employment rate, rise in the level of debts, and the economy of the country and the countries involved in trade with that country are affected.

RESEARCH OBJECTIVES

The objectives of this research paper are as follows:

- An analysis of The Great Depression of 1929, the worst financial crisis of the 20th century.
- To analyse systemic risks and how they impact an economy.

RESEARCH HYPOTHESIS

The research hypothesis in the paper is- the worst impact of the Great Depression was upon America.

DATA COLLECTION

For this research paper, data has been collected from secondary sources like journals and websites.

THE GREAT INDIAN DEPRESSION

FINANCIAL CRISIS

In a financial crisis, asset prices see a steep decline in value, businesses and consumers are unable to pay their debts, and financial institutions experience liquidity shortages.

A panic or a bank run is frequently connected with a financial crisis, in which investors sell assets or remove money from savings accounts because they believe the value of those assets will decline if they remain in the financial institution.

A financial crisis can also occur when a stock market crash occurs, a sovereign default occurs, or a currency crisis occurs. A financial crisis might affect only banks or it can affect an entire economy, a region's economy, or the entire world's economy.

A financial crisis can result from a variety of factors. In general, a crisis can emerge when institutions or assets are overvalued, and irrational or herd-like investment behaviour can add to the problem. When a bank failure is rumoured, for example, a rapid run of selloffs might result in reduced asset prices, pushing consumers to dump assets or make large savings withdrawals.

THE DEPRESSION OF 1929

A depression is a particularly severe sort of economic downturn. Depressions are defined by their length, abnormally high unemployment rate, decreased credit availability, shrinking production as buyers dry up and suppliers cut back on production and investment, a high number of bankruptcies, including sovereign debt defaults, significantly reduced trade and commerce (especially international trade), and highly volatile relative currency value (often due to currency devaluations). Price deflation, financial crises, and bank failures are other features of a depression that do not usually occur during a recession.

The Great Crisis was a worldwide economic depression that began in the United States in the 1930s and lasted until 1945. The Great Depression began in 1929 in most countries and lasted until the late 1930s in others. It was the twentieth century's longest, deepest, and most widespread slump in the twenty-first century.

The Great Depression began in the United States after a major drop in stock values that began around September 4, 1929, and resulted in the stock market crash of October 29, 1929, which made headlines around the world. The day is regarded so ominous that it is referred to as the Black Tuesday.

The rapid and sudden collapse of US stock market prices on October 29, 1929 is commonly seen as the start of the Great Depression. Some, however, disagree with this perspective, regarding the stock market crash as a consequence rather than a cause of the Great Depression.

The event that led to the great depression started with the rise in the level of the stock market in the early 1930s. Businesses started spending more and more on production of goods, i.e., mass production, in the initial half of the year. But there were many who had faced losses in the previous year, and thus, to make up for those, started cutting back on their expenditure. And upon this, America was facing a severe drought at that time. So eventually, in that year, the interest rates had dropped very low. The automobiles sales had declined. The cars that were so in demand one were not being purchased by the people. In general, there were many people who were unemployed and those who had jobs, their wages and incomes had been reduced. At first, the fall in the US economy was the cause that dragged down most other countries, and subsequently each country's internal shortcomings or strengths made things worse or better.

The United States' economy was damaged by the Great Depression of 1929. Half of all banks went bankrupt. Unemployment had climbed to 25%, and homelessness has increased. Housing prices dropped 30%, international trade fell 60%, and prices fell 10% per year. The stock market took 25 years to recover. In the first five years of the Great Depression, the GDP shrunk by half. This continued until 1939, when the preparations for World War II led to a growth of 8% in 1939 and 8.8% in 1940.

Year Unemployment Rate

1920 5.2%

1930 8.7%

1940 14.6%

1950 5.3%

1960 5.5%

1970 4.9%

Thus, The Great Depression had the following effects: industrial production fell by 50%, international trade fell by 30%, and investment dropped by 98%. Thus, it is safe to say that the Depression affected America more than any other country, because although other countries were affected, none of them were as badly affected as America. Thus the hypothesis stands correct.

<u>SYSTEMIC RISKS</u>

WHAT ARE SYSTEMIC RISKS?

A large-scale disruption affecting all financial institutions is not the same as systemic risk. Many financial entities, whether banks or non-banks, can be affected by big shared shocks. For example, there could be a significant drop in overall spending (all too common in smaller economies subject to terms of trade or export shocks). A negative outcome could result in increased loan losses and lower earnings for many institutions.

When an initial disturbance is transmitted via the networks of links that connect enterprises, families, and financial institutions with one another, a systemic risk arises, leading to the breakdown or degradation of these networks. It is the possibility that an event at a very small scale, let's say at the level of an individual bank, could trigger instability for an entire economy. It is sometimes known as a Domino Effect.

The concept of systemic risks came to be known after the Global Financial Crisis of 2008. To understand this in a very simple way, let us take the example of the Millennium Bridge in London. The bridge was opened in June, 2000, on the River Thames. Now what happened was that as soon as the bridge opened and people started to walk on it, it started swaying. And the reason behind this swaying was a mystery, even to the engineers who had constructed the bridge. Eventually, it earned the nickname of the Wobbly Bridge.

Finally, people understood the reason behind the swaying of the bridge. It was a reason that no one foresaw. It was a systemic risk. It is a well-known fact that when soldiers have to cross a bridge, they are asked to walk out of lock step, or else they would create a risk of wobbling of the bridge. But while the construction of the bridge, the engineers did not think about this because they thought that the people would be walking their different ways, i.e., not in lock step, so there would be no chance of the bridge wobbling.

So, when a gust of wind hit the bridge, the people were leaning against the movement, and to balance themselves started moving back and forth. And thus, unknowingly, the people on the bridge, without knowing each other and without talking to each other started moving in lock step, like an army of soldiers. Thus, causing the bridge to sway. The systemic event here was a little sway from the wind which caused the whole bridge to sway, with the people on it.

THE FLASH CRASH OF 2010

On 6th May, 2010, there was crash in the stock market, also known as the Flash Crash, in the United States market. It lasted for approximately 36 minutes. Due to a computer-based algorithm, the prices of shares fell very quickly and were very steep. But they were back up very quickly. It happened because a Kansas based man had an algorithm, that sold off more shares if there was much going on in the market. It decided to sell-off more shares as it saw action in the market. What happened because of this was that these shares that were sold off by this investor, were quickly purchased by traders. This cycle continued where these shares were being sold at lower prices and it continued. The algorithm noticed this and started selling more shares due to the action in the market. And so the prices started falling even more. This continued to such an extent that the prices went very low causing the crash of the market. The prices went so low that the investors of the market noticed this and finally brought the share prices back up.

It was concluded that the algorithm, individually, did the right thing, but when all the factors act together, can cause huge risks in the market. Thus, this was an instance of Systemic Risk in play. Systemic risks is caused by the interaction of people in financial market where they come together at the worst possible time and do the exact same thing, like sell off their assets at the same time and thereby causing the market to crash. Just like what the people did on the Millennium Bridge.

CONCLUSION

The impact that the global crises have on the countries cannot be avoided, no matter how prepared the country's financial system is. And although the countries are strengthening their financial systems and economies, to recover from the impact COVID-19 had, damage recovery takes time. This is so because the reason behind the crisis comes to be known only after the crisis occurs, thus it cannot be prevented in any way.

The only way to mitigate these crises is to be financially aware so as to avoid doing mistakes that lead to systemic risks, but then the question that arises is that what to do and what not to do to avoid risks. And that is a question that no one has an answer to yet.

CHAPTER TEN

THE PLIGHT OF A FILMMAKER: CENSORSHIP OF FILMS IN INDIA

Author: Radha B Narayanan, III year of B.A.,LL.B(Hons.) From PES University, Faculty of Law.

Co-author - 1: Pragathi U Bhat, III year of B.A.,LL.B(Hons.) From PES University, Faculty of Law.

Co-author -2: Nidhi N Anand, III year of B.A.,LL.B(Hons.) From PES University, Faculty of Law.

The expression of one's perceptions, values, and emotions is said to transpire through art. Films are a cogent means of expression because they appeal to the people by combining the auditory and visual senses. Films frequently contain the creators' viewpoints and beliefs. They have the ability to penetrate the viewer's mind and alter his perspective.

The freedom of speech and expression of Indian citizens is guaranteed by Article 19(1)(a) of the Constitution1. This constitutional clause embraces all artistic expression, including that of films. The freedom ensured by Article 19(1)(a) is bridled by the restrictions that can be imposed by the State to protect the integrity of the nation, the security of the nation, foreign relations, public order, decency and morality or to prevent contempt of court or defamation2. In India, the censorship of cinema has its origins in the ability to impose restrictions on the right to free expression by the State as mentioned in Article 19(2). The Cinematograph Act of 1952 created the Central Board of Film Certification (CBFC), also referred to as the "Censor Board," as a regulatory authority3. The Censor Board, empowered by Section 4 of the Cinematograph

Act,certifies feature films, short films, documentaries, or theater-based advertisements based on how appropriate they are for the audience. Each film is given one of four classifications by the Board: U for unrestricted public exhibition, A for adult audience only, U/A for movies that call for parental supervision for children under 12 years old, and S for special audiences only (such as the army).

With over 1250 films made each year, the Indian film industry is renowned around the world for its massive production of feature and short films.4 The issue about film censorship in India and whether it violates filmmakers' freedom of speech has arisen as a result of the recognition that cinema has the ability to influence people's ideas.Any kind of censorship might be seen as a barrier to innovation. The ideals of preserving and defending culture are frequently used to cloak unwarranted censorship, yet it is more often than not,that very culture that the filmmaker is attempting to expose and condemn. Films are not just made for amusement; they are also complex visual narratives that reflect the society in which they were created. Films endure increased censorship as they transition from being a light entertainment to being a watchdog of social issues. The impact of censorship is greater on films that are viewed in cinemas. Filmmakers now have the option to broadcast their movies online rather than in theaters owing to the existence of OTT (Over-the-Top) platforms, but these channels too are subject to censorship.

Films that are typically restricted in India deal with taboo subjects or expose societal aspects that we are not yet quite inclined to acknowledge, admit, or address. Any revisiting or reinterpretation of the past also often gets under the censorship radar owing to the fact that it is perceived as a threat to one's comfortably accepted position. To put it another way, the CBFC frequently considers the following factors when certifying a film: scenes that could cause racial unrest; scenes that glorify antisocial behaviors like drug abuse; scenes that offend religious communities; scenes that degrade women; scenes in biographical stories that distort the truth; scenes that depict sexuality explicitly without having any bearing on the plot; scenes that depict violence against children; and scenes that contain violence or gore. Some contemporary examples that can be cited to elaborate on this further are; the controversy surrounding the film 'Padmavat' where the Rajput community indignantly claimed that the film distorted historical facts, thus portraying their community in a bad light. The film was originally named 'Padmavati' and the CFBC agreed to give it clearance only if it was renamed and certain aspects of the films were modified along with a disclaimer that it was not based on historical events. Another film that was considered controversial was 'PK' because it was perceived to be a mockery of religion in a country where religious identity is of paramount significance. The film was intended to be a reflection of what religion has been reduced to but it went through rounds of debate in the censor board as allegations of the film hurting Hindu sentiments or promoting 'love-jihad' were brought forth. The film finally cleared the CBFC and was released but questions of stricter censorship and even a withdrawal of release was discussed post the release. Furthermore, the 2017 film 'Lipstick under my Burkha' faced the peril of being banned due to the explicit portrayal of women of different backgrounds exploring their sexuality and its take on the need for gender equality. After an appeal by the makers to the Film Certification Appellate Tribunal5,the film was allowed a release with an 'A' certificate and multiple cuts.

Off late there has been much discussion about the content that is produced on the OTT platforms which has been reported to be in violation of the nation's laws. The question that arises in such discussion is if the content should be monitored by a self regulatory body or a statutory body that has been specially established to censor the OTT content.

The Madhya Pradesh High Court in a PIL by Maatr Foundation 6 has advised that a pre-screening committee be constituted to regulate movies and television shows that are directly released on websites like Netflix and Hotstar. Therefore, it is clear that censorship of online series and digital content is very likely. However, a self-censorship agreement that has been signed by Netflix, Hotstar, Alt Balaji, Sony Liv, and other internet businesses forbids signatories from displaying any content that has been banned by Indian courts. The e-commerce behemoth's streaming service, Amazon Prime Video, has chosen not to abide by the code, arguing that the current laws are adequate.

The OTT platforms are not subject to any kind of regulation by the Union Ministry of Information and Broadcasting, Law and Justice, Electronics, Information and Technology, Telecom, or CBFC. The government views these platforms as middlemen over which they have no legal authority. However, in accordance with Rule 3(2)(b),(c), and (e) of the Information Technology (Intermediaries Guidance) Rules, 2011, intermediaries must use caution when showing, hosting, or publishing any obscene, pornographic, or illegal information and must not endanger minors. According to Rule 3(3), the intermediary is not permitted to knowingly host or start the transmission of such content.

One of the most recent issues surrounding OTT's was the John Oliver show on Hotstar, where he actively criticized the majority government and its actions and the show was further blocked on Hotstar. A similar incident occurred on Hasan Minaj's show that dealt with Lok Sabha Elections, 2019 and was highly criticized later.

The Supreme Court of India considers censorship to be "essential" 7 when there is a chance that certain aspects of the movie can elicit strong feelings and emotions from particular groups in society. The Court also acknowledges the influence that movies have as a powerfully visual medium with high rates of recall. In India, judicial censorship has a lengthy history. The State and the Judiciary have traditionally paid undue attention to movies.This approach can be best described from an excerpt nearly 50 years ago that challenged the constitutionality of censorship. In the landmark case of S. Rangarajan v P. Jagjivan Ram case8 the court held that,

"Movies motivate thought and action and assure a high degree of attention and retention. It makes its impact by simultaneously arousing the visual and aural senses... The focusing of an intense light on a screen with the dramatizing of facts and opinion makes the ideas more effective. The combination of act and speech, sight and sound in semi-darkness of the theatre with elimination of all distracting ideas will have an impact in the minds of spectators."

In K.A. Abbas v. Union of India9, the CBFC denied the unrestrained screening of the documentary, 'A tale of four cities'. The reasoning given for this was that parts of the movie were shot in the Red Light Areas of Bombay. The CBFC asked the petitioner to edit the scenes shot in the Red Light Areas as a condition to permit the release of the film. The petitioner, displeased with the decision pronounced by the board decided to file a suit in the Supreme Court contending that the CBFC violated his Freedom of Speech and Expression which was granted under Article 19(1)(a). The apex court held that pre-censorship of cinema was constitutionally valid. The Apex Court further upheld that the censorship of films to safeguard the order and morality of the society is justified.

In any discussion on the constitutional validity of censorship, it is pertinent to examine if the judiciary possesses the necessary authority to consider the merits of the adjustments recommended by the CBFC. Justice Black's comment in the landmark case Kingsley International Pictures

Corpn. v. Regents of the University of the State of New York10 gives us a greater understanding of the role of the Judiciary in censorship of films.

He observed that:

... judges possess no special expertise providing exceptional competency to set standards and to supervise the private morals of the Nation. In addition, the Justices of this Court seem especially unsuited to make the kind of value judgments—as to what movies are good or bad for local communities....

While the CBFC has the authority to impose adjustments and cuts on any portions of a film that break its standards, this is frequently done by distorting the meaning of the picture to make it appear as though a breach has occurred when it may not have. Filmmakers must be careful and consider all possible angles from which their work could be dissected and criticised. In 2021, the Ministry of Information and Broadcasting proposed the Cinematograph (Amendment) Bill 2021, one of the aspects of which is the Central Government's power to order a recertification of a film that has already been certified by the CBFC. Filmmakers now face an added layer of potential censoring which could limit their ability to express themselves creatively.

Organisations like the CBFC take it upon themselves to define what is right for the general population of the country. This not only restricts the narrative of the filmmaker but also restricts the stories the people of the state can consume. On account of the unwarranted restrictions and censorship, people lose access to diverse perspectives. This limits the fundamental freedom of expression and thus goes against our basic constitutional tenets. Film censorship by state agencies like the CBFC is viewed as a flagrant violation of Article 19(1)(a). Every citizen is bestowed with the freedom of speech and expression in our constitution. When the ability to express is shackled by unjustified restrictions, the filmmaker will not be in a position to communicate the message. Justice Lodha's comment "if you don't like it don't watch it"11 precisely defines how the craft of motion pictures are to be dealt with. The Shyam Benegal Committee constituted in 2016 had recommended the abolition of the CBFC. But the transfer of powers from the CBFC to the Judiciary would be far worse. The Judiciary is devoid of any jurisdiction with respect to these matters. As a society, we've developed a fear of expressing things that may be against the norm. How can we analyse different perspectives without engaging in conversation? We find ourselves in a predicament when we prefer censorship to content analysis due to our fear of critically exploring topics. The CBFC should uphold meticulous standards to appropriately certify the films so that it reaches the suitable standards but any unwarranted and unjustified cuts by the Board on baseless assumptions and unfounded claims should be impermissible. In the authors' opinion the Central Government should develop comprehensive guidelines that permit scenes depicting violence or abuse or any other unsettling matter only if it is of significance to the plot. Any unnecessary depiction of such content should be discouraged. Therefore, although the State is constitutionally empowered by Article 19(2) to place restrictions in the form of censorship, the State should keep in mind the grounds specified in the Constitution and should not shackle the creative freedom of the filmmakers on prejudiced claims.

CHAPTER ELEVEN

PATENTS IN ENERGY SECTOR: SPECIAL EMPHASIS ON SUSTAINABLE RESOURCES

Author: Aditi Arora, III year of B.B.A.,LL.B. from Vivekananda Institute of Professional Studies

Abstract

The paper outlines the importance of developing sustainable energy technologies and securing patent protection for preventing the depletion of all the non-renewable natural resources on our planet. Initially the paper stresses upon the highly imperative promotion of innovation in the energy sector to foster better utilisation of solar, wind, hydro, tidal and other renewables available abundantly on the planet.

Then it explains briefly, the different types of renewable energy resources that can be exploited endlessly without the fear of depletion. The paper tries to motivate the innovators to come up with novel technologies to utilise renewable resources for an environment alternative by providing the latest examples of inventions in different sectors of sustainable growth.

It further proceeds to highlight the role of patents in analysing and forecasting the growth of innovation in the energy sector and simultaneously boosting innovations. Then with the help of statistics, the trends in sustainable energy patents is analysed and thereafter compared with the all-over patent database over the past decade.

The paper makes an effort to provide a fair picture of the current scenario of the green patents filing worldwide and thereby indicating the steps taken towards promoting sustainable energy. It then classifies the patentable innovations involving renewable energy into three broad categories of technologies in: mature market stage, trending in the market and venture stage.

Further, it goes on to clarify the Indian stance on renewable energy innovations and initiatives taken up by the Indian government to accelerate growth in the said field followed by challenges to sustainable development and patenting. To conclude, the paper discusses the impact of the regulation policies and movements to encourage green patents and therefore sustainable energy innovations to urge global sustainable growth.

Introduction

As Tim Wirth once said, "Energy is essential for development and sustainable energy is essential for sustainable development", we realise that with the planet on the verge of depleting all its natural resources in the urge of generating power, it is the need of the hour to look for alternative sustainable technologies. According to the extrapolated projections of 2017 by IEA it is estimated that by the end of 2040, the world will require up to 30% more energy as compared to today's consumption. To gain a better understanding on sustainable development in the energy sector, it is imperative for the following generation to become aware of the different types of renewable energy resources and their corresponding technological developments to take up the baton. Innovation is the only way to tackle the pressing need. It is also imperative to track the innovations to update and encourage upcoming professionals. The most prominent methodology to analyse the growth of sustainable developments in the energy sector is to observe the patent trends over the years which indicates the amount of innovations taking place in the desired sector. Databases such as the IPC green inventory keep a record of the patent information regarding the Environmentally Sound Technologies (ESTs) as listed by UNFCCC. Analysing the data collected from all these National and International Inventories can provide a fair picture of the global scenario in this direction.

Especially in India, the future prosperity depends on the achievability of affordable and clean energy fuels and it would take an even longer time now after restoring the disruptions caused by Covid-19 pandemic. Although prior to the worldwide pandemic, India's energy demand was projected to increase by 50% between 2019 and 2030, but instead it is now around 35%, but due to the economic downfall, the Indian households are falling back to more polluting and lesser efficient fuels and it has also hampered the growth rate of innovations and green patents.

Role of Patents in Innovation

Patents provide a yard-stick to measure innovations and standards for the deployment of renewable energy technologies for the stakeholders by playing the following roles:-

· Incentivization: Patent registration fairly remunerate the inventors by giving them exclusive rights to use, distribute, licence and raise profits to compensate their efforts and costs incurred in the innovating process for a limited period of time i.e. twenty years after the date of patent application filing. Patents simply grant sole ownership and enjoyment rights which facilitates monopoly to cover the investment and labour for a stipulated time frame.

· Increases knowledge base: Publication of an invention for patent allows the general public to obtain new technology and inspirations to innovate further while avoiding reinventing similar innovations.

· Attracts Investors: Registered patents are easier to transfer and licence and facilitates a smoother flow of business. It helps in attracting investors by acting as a strong intangible asset

· Encourages Innovation: it inspires present and future specialists to innovate more by offering lucrative benefits of patent protection

· Analysing and Forecasting Growth Trends in Each Sector: Patents act as a measure of research output, containing information on the development of new technologies. It indicates individual growth in each sector respectively and gives a fair idea of the fields that lack innovations and therefore has a scope for technological development!

· Foundation for other innovations: Other than public declaration of technical know-how, the off-patent technologies act as a foundation for developing new and upcoming inventions which are modified and enhanced with the help of recent advancements and suitably adapting them to local conditions.

Patent documents provide insights on state-of-the-art technological information, legal and business information, latest trends in innovation and a guidance to policy makers and inverstors to make an informed decision. In addition to the public declaration of the patent information, the databases also provide various tools for retrieval of relevant search results for researchers

Major Renewable Energy Resources and Sustainable Innovations

1. Solar Energy: Sunlight is one of the most abundant resources on earth. It is a cleaner, affordable and inexhaustible form of energy which provides greater returns on investment, with solar panels being easy to set-up and provides a much better and cheaper alternative to household electricity. At present, solar energy is growing at the rate of 13.6%. In India, over the recent 5 years, solar power capacity has accelerated at an average rate of around 60%.

Latest inventions in generating solar energy and its utilisation include:-

- Inventions in Photovoltaics such as devices adapted for the conversion of radiation energy into electrical energy, assemblies of a plurality of solar cells, silicon; single-crystal growth, regulating to the maximum power available from solar cells and charging batteries etc.
- Use of solar heat for domestic hot water systems and space heating etc.
- propulsion of vehicles using solar power
- roof covering aspects of energy collecting devices

2. Wind Energy: With wind turbines being a common sighting on farms and ranches, the benefits of generating power through the cost effective technologies regarding wind energy are becoming more evident.Wind energy technologies are growing at the rate of 16.7% each year whereas the Indian growth rate in wind power generation caopacity has increased around 10%.

Innovations in wind energy sector include:-

- Structural aspects of wind turbines
- Structural association of electric generator with mechanical driving motor
- Propulsion of vehicles using wind power

3. Hydro Energy: Hydroelectricity is amongst the most cost effective and commercially developed sources of energy and generated mostly by building damsand water reservoirs. However, many countries including India are over dependent on hydropower for their meeting their consumption, According to the Council on Energy, Environment and Water (CEEW), it is estimated that India must generate at least 83% of its electricity from non-hydropower renewable energy sources to reach net-zero in carbon emmisions by 2050.

Innovations in Hydro Energy sector includes:-

- Water-power plants
- Machines or engines for liquids
- Propulsion of marine vessels using energy derived from water movement
- Tidal or wave powerplants

4. Geothermal Energy: It involves a process of generating energy by tapping the underground heat. It is prominently used for bathing and home heating appliances. The global geothermal electricity market is expected to grow to \$6.06 billion by the end of 2022 at a growth rate of 9.6% from last year.

Innovations in Geothermal Energy includes:-

- Use of geothermal heat
- Production of mechanical power from geothermal energy

Sustainable Energy Patents from the <u>IPC Green Inventory</u>:-

Category	Topic
Alternative Energy Production	<ul><li>Bio-fuels</li><li>Integrated gasification combined cycle (IGCC)</li><li>Fuel cells</li><li>Pyrolysis or gasification of biomass</li><li>Harnessing energy from manmade waste</li><li>Ocean thermal energy conversion (OTEC)</li><li>Other production or use of heat, not derived from combustion, e.g. natural heat</li><li>Using waste heat</li><li>Devices for producing mechanical power from muscle energy</li></ul>
Transportation	<ul><li>Vehicles in general (e.g. hybrid vehicles, electric propulsion)</li><li>Vehicles other than rail vehicles</li><li>Rail vehicles</li><li>Marine vessel propulsion</li><li>Cosmonautic vehicles using solar energy</li></ul>
Energy conservation	<ul><li>Storage of electrical energy</li><li>Power supply circuitry</li><li>Measurement of electricity consumption</li><li>Storage of thermal energy</li><li>Low energy lighting</li><li>Thermal building insulation, in general</li><li>Recovering mechanical energy</li></ul>
Waste Management	<ul><li>Waste disposal</li><li>Treatment of waste</li><li>Reusing waste materials</li><li>Pollution control</li></ul>
Nuclear power generation	<ul><li>Nuclear engineering (e.g. Fusion reactors, nuclear fission reactors, nuclear power plants)</li><li>Gas turbine power plants using heat source of nuclear origin</li></ul>

<u>Trends in sustainable energy patents</u>

Green energy patents have observed exponential growth up till 2013 followed by a period of deceleration and the minor decline in green energy technology innovation. However patents in energy conservation technology and green transportation technology have shown a constant and steady pace. The investment in renewable energy technologies is now more than ever before which is evident from the proliferation of wind turbines and solar cells spread across the landscape. According to a <u>2019 report on Global Trends in Renewable Energy Investment</u> it was claimed that 26.3% of the total electricity produced around the globe is renewable energy with a total of USD 2.6 trillion investment in the past decade! Although the investment statistics do not provide the accurate measurement of the growth in this sector due to the gradual cost reduction of solar and wind power plants installation which is also a positive indicator.

Over 60% of all the green energy patents around the world are highly concentrated in only four countries that are: (Japan, U.S., Germany and China)[i]. The growth rate of green patent filings in the energy sector in China has increased extraordinarily since the past decade, making it the second highest with regards to green energy patent families. However majority of the extraordinary growth in green patents have been filed at the home country i.e. China and not internationally under PCT. On the contrary, the leading inventors of green energy technologies, Japan and United States have experienced a fall in the number of green patents since 2011.

India has also shown a shift from the conventional resources of energy to renewable resources to support the trend of sustainable development. Photovoltaic has been the topmost technology to secure almost 6000 patents in India as compared to 10000 other patent applications registered in different domains relating to renewable energy, such as: wind energy, conversion process of hydrostatic pressure into electrical energy, hydro wind electric power generation system and solar thermal appliances for domestic applicability etc.

In the 2018 edition of the Global Innovation Index, themed as 'Energizing the World with Innovation' it was stated that a much higher level of innovation is required in the energy supply side as compared to the demand side. In other words, the inclination towards alternative sustainable energy resources requires greater level of technological advancements as compared to smart cities, efficient transportation and mobility and optimization of energy systems which includes establishing smart grids and novel, advanced technologies for storing energy.

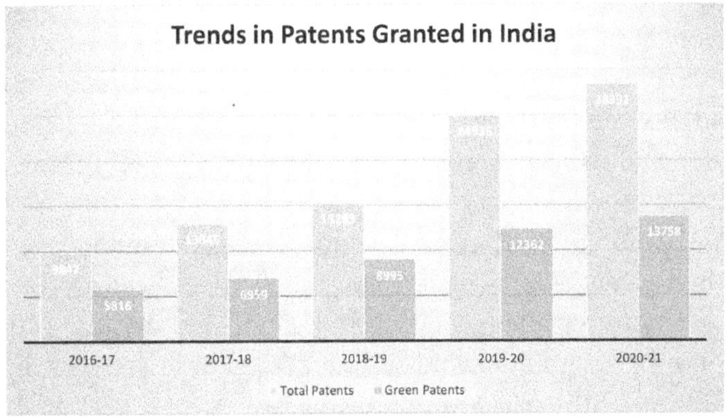

Source: Commerce and Industry Ministry

The data depicts that on an average almost half of the total registered patents in India are green energy patents concerning waste management, alternative energy production, transportation technologies and energy conservation etc.

Classification of patentable innovations involving renewable energy

It is essential to bifurcate the inventions and the corresponding patents into separate categories to better understand their evolution, market share, scope of development and area-specific requirement. Thus there are three broad categories of patentable technologies on the basis of their status of growth in the market:-

1. Technologies in Mature market stage: This category includes the innovations that are introduced in an existing mature market and there are many patents already registered in that field. Hence the new patent applications have to be cautiously registered so as to not infringe any existing patents. For example solar, wind and tidal energy technologies, hybrid vehicles etc. fall under mature and developed market stage.

2. Technologies trending in the market: The technologies that have just entered the market and are therefore popular and trending comes under this stage. The commercial viability and future success can be analysed through the inventions in their trending stage. These renewable technologies include smart grids, biofuels and ethanol based fuels

3. Technologies at the venture stage: At the venture stage technologies are mostly undergoing the research or planning step in order to enter the commercial market. These technology substantially have an untapped potential. They are freshly introduced and have endless opportunities for new inventions and innovations. Renewable energy such as wireless power transmission and nano-materials are few examples of technologies in their venture stage.

India's Position in Promoting Sustainable Development

India, being a developing nation, constantly undergoing industrialisation and organisation which generates of humungous demand for energy. However the per capita demand of energy is still lesser than half of the global average with wide variations across the states and between metropolitan cities and rural areas. The reliability of energy supply and its affordability remains one of the primary concerns for India's consumers. In a research report published by WIPO[i], India is the largest contribution to energy demand growth, amounting up to 30%. Thus switching to sustainable alternatives and promoting innovations in the renewable energy sector is crucial for the country. India, being an environmentally committed nation, is constantly taking up initiatives to foster and support the global goals (SDGs) introduced by United Nations. NITI Ayog has recently released a report on Renewables Integration in India, 2021 in collaboration with the Indian Economic Service (IES). The report focusses on suggesting methods for maximising the production and value of solar and wind power in its electricity system. Other than this, the report also brings forth a few distinctive regulatory policies for incentivizing renewable energy resources and facilitating their accommodation into the energy system with greater ease and flexibility.

India has a flourishing industry in Low-Carbon Environmental Goods and Services (LCEGS). The reports on LCEGS play an important role of fulfilling the gap due to the lack of an accepted classification system and statistical base for the measurement of environmental and low-carbon focussed activities within the country. It is also an initiative towards achieving the challenge of producing robust measures and indicators related to the green economy as a whole thereby essentially enabling policy makers to make the concept of green growth operational and providing proper International tools to measure and monitor economic effect.

The central government has introduced an array of initiative including strategic partnership with Denmark, production linked incentives to solar power manufacturers and the renewable energy technologies push by the Department of Science and Technology. The telecommunication Industry has also issued directions to the Telecom Service Providers for using sustainable energy technologies.

However despite of all the efforts, India is lacking at the energy front due to its over dependency on three fuels: coal, oil and solid biomass which take decades to replenish if not centuries and fulfils around 80% of the energy needs of the country!

The recent pandemic has also introduced global crisis in all the sectors. According to a report on India Energy Outlook, published by the International Energy Agency, due to the Covid-19 pandemic and a series of lockdowns and related restrictions, there has been a 5% decline in India's energy demand in 2020, with petroleum and coal use suffering the major fall. The pandemic also affected investments in the energy sector, with a fall of about 15% in 2020

Challenges to Sustainable Growth and Patenting

The predominant hurdle to attaining sustainable growth by rigorous innovation spree is posed by the recent Covid-19 pandemic which hampered the research and development in energy sector, mojaorly declined investment capacity, distracted the government policies to other prssing nessecities, lowered the pace of documentation for application and granting of patents, reduced the per capity income and affordability of cleaner fuels by renewable resources and much more! All the countries around the world are struggling to restore the damages caused in the recent years but still there is a long road to normality.

The other challenge in switching to alternative fuels is finding the appropriate geographical conditions for generating energy from renewable resources such as tidal, hydro and wind which requires extensive set-up and abundance of that resource whereas coal and petroleum are easily transported and stored as pcr requirement. Also, most of the renewable energy resources are variable in nature and the amount of energy generated through them is uneven and uncertain throughout the year and across regions.

It has also been observed that the transfer of technologies in renewable energy faces difficulties in the field of transaction and assurance cost. Many a times, the transfer does not succeed due to a larger transaction cost of the technology involved.

Government policies and subsidies can also play a major role in determining the innovation growth. It also includes the intervention of Competition Laws, Privatisation, government sponsored R&D, decline in oil and petroleum prices leading to lesser incentives for sustainable alternatives.

In contrast, the difficulties in patenting mostly relates to the territorial nature of patent rights which provides protection only in the country we are applying in and different countries having their specific classification schemes and regulation policies. The diffusion of technological advancements across countries is more often complicated than not. The policy makers and investors find it hard to analyse the patent databases due to this non uniformity and different classification systems yielding different results of patent search..

However, the complete picture of determinants for the green energy patenting slowdown is not entirely clear.

<u>Conclusion</u>

According to Charles Darwin's theories, our only chance of survival is to adapt to the changing environment and for that we need a major shift to green resources for power. From the aforementioned global statistics and report, it can certainly be inferred that growth in sustainable development technologies cannot be overlooked and constant cycle of innovations and patenting is only way to move ahead with time! The data shows the growth in each sector and makes us realise that even though we are steadily inclined towards sustainable environment, we are still majorly dependent on tapping fossil fuels and slowly depreciating sources of energy for meeting our demands. The patent databases are great way to spotlight the areas of lesser growth that are lacking innovations to survive in today's conditions. The global warming, drastic environmental changes and worldwide pandemic are nature's warning to human kind for mending their ways to a sustainable future and inventions are the only way to accelerate development by effectively utilising renewable resources such as solar, tidal, wind and hydro, just enough to keep pace with what the future!

Concluding with the famous words: "Sustainable Development is the masterful balance of meeting our own needs without jeopardizing the future generations' ability to do the same"

[i] Supra 4, pg. 3

[i] Rivera León, Kyle Bergquist, Sacha Wunsch-Vincent, Ning Xu and Kunihiko Fushimi. "Measuring innovation in energy technologies: green

patents as captured by WIPO's IPC green inventory." Economic Research Working Paper No. 44, pg. 10,

WIPO, https://www.wipo.int/edocs/pubdocs/en/wipo_pub_econstat_wp_44.pdf

<u>Author's Bio</u>

Aditi Arora, a 3rd year student at VIPS is an ambitious young adult filled with innovative ideas and a creative approach. She is highly intrigued by the nuances of IPR and aligning fields of corporate law.

LinkedIn: https://www.linkedin.com/in/aditi-arora-4b0530201

www.ingramcontent.com/pod-product-compliance
Lightning Source LLC
Chambersburg PA
CBHW051345150726
48000CB00003B/1049